SWAMI SRI YUKTESWAR

ज्ञानावतार स्वामी श्रीयुक्तेश्वरेण प्रणीतम्

कैवल्यदर्शनम्

Kaivalya Darsanam

The Holy Science

By
Jnanavatar Swami Sri Yukteswar Giri

Self-Realization Fellowship
FOUNDED 1920
Paramahansa Yogananda

Authorized by the International Publications Council of
SELF-REALIZATION FELLOWSHIP
3880 San Rafael Avenue • Los Angeles, CA 90065-3298

In 1920, Swami Sri Yukteswar sent to the United States his chief disciple, Paramahanasa Yogananda, to carry to the West India's ancient science of Yoga. Paramahansaji founded Self-Realization Fellowship at the behest of his Guru to serve as the instrument for the worldwide dissemination of the Kriya Yoga teachings of the SRF line of Gurus. The Self-Realization Fellowship name and emblem (shown above) appear on all SRF books, recordings, and other publications, assuring the reader that a work originates with the society established by Paramahansa Yogananda and faithfully conveys his teachings.

Library of Congress Catalog Card Number: 77-88199
ISBN 0-87612-051-6
Printed in the United States of America
10479-87654

CONTENTS

Photographs

FOREWORD

Prophets of all lands and ages have succeeded in their God-quest. Entering a state of true illumination, *nirbikalpa samadhi,* these saints have realized the Supreme Reality behind all names and forms. Their wisdom and spiritual counsel have become the scriptures of the world. These, although outwardly differing by reason of the variegated cloaks of words, are all expressions—some open and clear, others hidden or symbolic—of the same basic truths of Spirit.

My *gurudeva,* Jnanavatar* Swami Sri Yukteswar (1855–1936) of Serampore, was eminently fitted to discern the underlying unity between the scriptures of Christianity and of *Sanatan Dharma.* Placing the holy texts on the spotless table of his mind, he was able to dissect them with the scalpel of intuitive reasoning, and to separate interpolations and wrong interpretations of scholars from the truths as originally given by the prophets.

It is owing to Jnanavatar Swami Sri Yukteswar's unerring spiritual insight that it now becomes possible, through this book, to establish a fundamental harmony between the difficult biblical book, *Revelation,* and the *Sankhya* philosophy of India.

* "Incarnation of Wisdom"; from Sanskrit *jnana,* "wisdom," and *avatara,* "divine incarnation." *(Publisher's Note)*

As my *gurudeva* has explained in his introduction, these pages were written by him in obedience to a request made by Babaji, the holy *gurudeva* of Lahiri Mahasaya, who in turn was the *gurudeva* of Sri Yukteswar. I have written about the Christlike lives of these three great masters in my book, *Autobiography of a Yogi.**

The Sanskrit *sutras* set forth in *The Holy Science* will shed much light on the Bhagavad Gita as well as on other great scriptures of India.

Paramahansa Yogananda

249 Dwapara (A.D. 1949)

* See page 110. *(Publisher's Note)*

PREFACE

By W.Y. Evans-Wentz, M.A., D.Litt., D.Sc.
Author of
The Tibetan Book of the Dead,
Tibet's Great Yogi Milarepa,
Tibetan Yoga and Secret Doctrines, etc.

"It has been my privilege to meet...Sri Yukteswar Giri. A likeness of the venerable saint appeared as part of the frontispiece of my *Tibetan
Yoga and Secret Doctrines.* It was at Puri, in Orissa,
on the Bay of Bengal, that I encountered Sri Yukteswar. He was then the head of a quiet *ashrama*
near the seashore there and was chiefly occupied
in the spiritual training of a group of youthful
disciples.... Sri Yukteswar was of gentle mien and
voice, of pleasing presence, and worthy of the
veneration that his followers spontaneously ac-
corded to him. Every person who knew him,
whether of his own community or not, held him in
the highest esteem. I vividly recall his tall, straight,
ascetic figure, robed in the saffron-colored garb of
one who has renounced worldly quests, as he stood
at the entrance of the hermitage to give me wel-
come. He had chosen as his place of earthly abode
the holy city of Puri, whither multitudes of pious
Hindus, representative of every province of India,

come daily on pilgrimage to the famed Temple of Jagannath, "Lord of the World." It was at Puri that Sri Yukteswar closed his mortal eyes, in 1936, to the scenes of this transitory state of being and passed on, knowing that his incarnation had been carried to a triumphant completion.

"I am glad, indeed, to be able to record this testimony to the high character and holiness of Sri Yukteswar."

Swami Sri Yukteswar and Paramahansa Yogananda,
Calcutta, 1935

Swami Sri Yukteswar and Paramahansa Yogananda during religious festival held at Sri Yukteswar's Serampore ashram, December 1935. The following day, the great Guru summoned his beloved disciple and transferred to him the responsibility for his ashrams and spiritual work: "My task on earth is finished; you must carry on . . . . I leave everything in your hands."

THE
HOLY SCIENCE

INTRODUCTION

चतुर्नवत्युत्तर शतवर्षे गते द्वापरस्य प्रयागक्षेत्रे ।
सदर्शनविज्ञानमन्वयार्थे परमगुरुराजस्याज्ञान्तु प्राप्य ॥
कड़ारवंश्यप्रियनाथस्वामिकादम्बिनीक्षेत्रनाथात्मजेन ।
हिताय विश्वस्य विदग्धतुष्टयें प्रणीतं दर्शनं कैवल्यमेतत् ॥

[This *Kaivalya Darsanam* (exposition of Final
Truth) has been written by Priya Nath Swami,*
son of Kshetranath and Kadambini of the Karar
family.

At the request in Allahabad of the Great
Preceptor (Mahavatar Babaji) near the end of the
194th year of the present Dwapara Yuga, this
exposition has been published for the benefit of
the world.]

The purpose of this book is to show as clearly
as possible that there is an essential unity in all
religions; that there is no difference in the truths
inculcated by the various faiths; that there is but
one method by which the world, both external
and internal, has evolved; and that there is but
one Goal admitted by all scriptures. But this basic
truth is one not easily comprehended. The dis-

* In 1894, when this book was written, Babaji gave the author the
title of "Swami." He was later formally initiated into the Swami
Order by the *Mahant* (monastery head) of Buddh Gaya, Bihar,
and took the monastic name of Sri Yukteswar. He belonged to the
Giri ("mountain") branch of the Swami Order. *(Publisher's Note)*

cord existing between the different religions, and the ignorance of men, make it almost impossible to lift the veil and have a look at this grand verity. The creeds foster a spirit of hostility and dissension; ignorance widens the gulf that separates one creed from another. Only a few specially gifted persons can rise superior to the influence of their professed creeds and find absolute unanimity in the truths propagated by all great faiths.

The object of this book is to point out the harmony underlying the various religions, and to help in binding them together. This task is indeed a herculean one, but at Allahabad I was entrusted with the mission by a holy command. Allahabad, the sacred *Prayaga Tirtha*, the place of confluence of the Ganges, Yamuna, and Saraswati rivers, is a site for the congregation of worldly men and of spiritual devotees at the time of *Kumbha Mela*. Worldly men cannot transcend the mundane limit in which they have confined themselves; nor can spiritual devotees, having once renounced the world, deign to come down and mix themselves in its turmoil. Yet men who are wholly engrossed in earthly concerns stand in definite need of help and guidance from those holy beings who bring light to the race. So a place there must be where union between the two sets is possible. *Tirtha* affords such a meeting place. Situated as it is on the beach of the world, storms and buffets touch it not; the *sadhus* (ascetics) with a message for the benefit of humanity find a *Kumbha Mela* to be an ideal place to impart instruction to those who can heed it.

A message of such a nature was I chosen to propagate when I paid a visit to the *Kumbha Mela* being held at Allahabad in January 1894. As I was walking along the bank of the Ganges, I was summoned by a man and was afterwards honored by an interview with a great holy person, Babaji, the *gurudeva* of my own guru, Lahiri Mahasaya, of Banaras. This holy personage at the *Kumbha Mela* was thus my own *paramguruji maharaj,* * though this was our first meeting.

During my conversation with Babaji, we spoke of the particular class of men who now frequent these places of pilgrimage. I humbly suggested that there were men greater by far in intelligence than most of those then present, men living in distant parts of the world—Europe and America—professing different creeds, and ignorant of the real significance of the *Kumbha Mela.* They were men fit to hold communion with the spiritual devotees, so far as intelligence is concerned; yet such intellectual men in foreign lands were, alas, wedded in many cases to rank materialism. Some of them, though famous for their investigations in the realms of science and philosophy, do not recognize the essential unity in reli-

---

* *Paramguru,* literally, "guru beyond," hence the guru of one's guru. The suffix *ji* denotes respect. *Maharaj,* "great king," is a title often added to the names of exceptional spiritual personages. *(Publisher's Note)*

gion. The professed creeds serve as nearly insurmountable barriers that threaten to separate mankind forever.

My *paramguruji maharaj* Babaji smiled and, honoring me with the title of Swami, imposed on me the task of this book. I was chosen, I do not know the reason why, to remove the barriers and to help in establishing the basic truth in all religions.

The book is divided into four sections, according to the four stages in the development of knowledge. The highest aim of religion is *Atmajnanam,* Self-knowledge. But to attain this, knowledge of the external world is necessary. Therefore the first section of the book deals with वेद (*veda*) the gospel, and seeks to establish fundamental truths of creation and to describe the evolution and involution of the world.

All creatures, from the highest to the lowest in the link of creation, are found eager to realize three things: Existence, Consciousness, and Bliss. These purposes or goals are the subject for discussion in the second section of the book. The third section deals with the method of realizing the three purposes of life. The fourth section discusses the revelations which come to those who have traveled far to realize the three ideals of life and who are very near their destination.

The method I have adopted in the book is first to enunciate a proposition in Sanskrit terms of the Oriental sages, and then to explain it by reference to the holy scriptures of the West. In this way I have tried my best to show that there is no real discrepancy, much less any real conflict, between the teachings of the East and the West. Written as the book is, under the inspiration of my *paramgurudeva,* and in a Dwapara Age of rapid development in all departments of knowledge, I hope that the significance of the book will not be missed by those for whom it is meant.

A short discussion with mathematical calculation of the *yugas* or ages will explain the fact that the present age for the world is Dwapara Yuga, and that 194 years of the Yuga have now (A.D. 1894) passed away, bringing a rapid development in man's knowledge.

We learn from Oriental astronomy that moons revolve around their planets, and planets turning on their axes revolve with their moons round the sun; and the sun, with its planets and their moons, takes some star for its dual and revolves round it in about 24,000 years of our earth—a celestial phenomenon which causes the backward movement of the equinoctial points around the zodiac. The sun also has another motion by which it revolves round a grand center called *Vishnunabhi,* which is the seat of the creative power, *Brahma,* the universal magnetism. *Brahma* regulates *dharma,* the mental virtue of the internal world.

When the sun in its revolution round its dual comes to the place nearest to this grand center, the seat of *Brahma* (an event which takes place when the Autumnal Equinox comes to the first point of Aries), *dharma,* the mental virtue, becomes so much developed that man can easily comprehend all, even the mysteries of Spirit.

The Autumnal Equinox will be falling, at the beginning of the twentieth century, among the fixed stars of the Virgo constellation, and in the early part of the Ascending Dwapara Yuga.*

After 12,000 years, when the sun goes to the place in its orbit which is farthest from *Brahma,* the grand center (an event which takes place when the Autumnal Equinox is on the first point of Libra), *dharma,* the mental virtue, comes to such a reduced state that man cannot grasp anything beyond the gross material creation. Again, in the same manner, when the sun in its course of revolution begins to advance toward the place nearest to the grand center, *dharma,* the mental virtue, begins to develop; this growth is gradually completed in another 12,000 years.

Each of these periods of 12,000 years brings a complete change, both externally in the material world, and internally in the intellectual or electric world, and is called one of the Daiva Yugas or Electric Couple. Thus, in a period of 24,000 years, the sun completes the revolution around its

* See diagram on page 9.

DIAGRAM

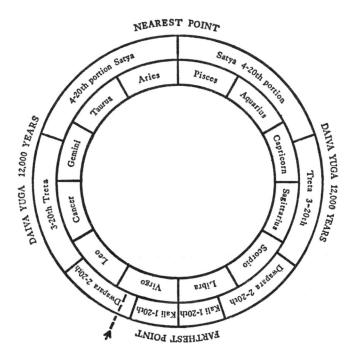

Virgo is the sign opposite Pisces. The Autumnal Equinox is now falling in Virgo; the opposite point, the Vernal Equinox, is perforce now falling in Pisces. Western metaphysicians, who consider the Vernal Equinox to have chief significance, therefore say the world is now in the "Piscean Age."

The Equinoxes have a retrograde movement in the constellations; hence, when the Equinoxes leave Pisces-Virgo, they will enter Aquarius-Leo. According to Swami Sri Yukteswarji's theory, the world entered the Pisces-Virgo Age in A.D. 499, and will enter the Aquarius-Leo Age two thousand years later, in A.D. 2499. *(Publisher's Note)* dual and finishes one electric cycle consisting of 12,000 years in an ascending arc and 12,000 years in a descending arc.

Development of *dharma,* the mental virtue, is but gradual and is divided into four different stages in a period of 12,000 years. The time of 1200 years during which the sun passes through a 1/20th portion of its orbit (*see* Diagram) is called Kali Yuga. *Dharma,* the mental virtue, is then in its first stage and is only a quarter developed; the human intellect cannot comprehend anything beyond the gross material of this ever-changing creation, the external world.

The period of 2400 years during which the sun passes through the 2/20th portion of its orbit is called Dwapara Yuga. *Dharma,* the mental virtue, is then in the second stage of development and is but half complete; the human intellect can then comprehend the fine matters or electricities and their attributes which are the creating principles of the external world.

The period of 3600 years during which the sun passes through the 3/20th part of its orbit is called Treta Yuga. *Dharma,* the mental virtue, is then in the third stage; the human intellect becomes able to comprehend the divine magnetism, the source of all electrical forces on which the creation depends for its existence.

The period of 4800 years during which the sun passes through the remaining 4/20th portion of its orbit is called Satya Yuga. *Dharma,* the mental virtue, is then in its fourth stage and completes its full development; the human intellect can comprehend all, even God the Spirit beyond this visible world.

Manu, a great *rishi* (illumined sage) of Satya Yuga, describes these Yugas more clearly in the following passage from his *Samhita:*

चत्वार्याहुः सहस्राणि वर्षाणान्तु कृतं युगम् ।
तस्य तावच्छती सन्ध्या सन्ध्यांशश्च तथाविधः ॥
इतरेषु ससन्ध्येषु ससन्ध्यांशेषु च त्रिषु ।
एकापायेन वर्त्तन्ते सहस्राणि शतानि च ॥
यदेतत् परिसंख्यातमादावेव चतुर्युगम् ।
एतद् द्वादशसाहस्रं देवानां युगमुच्यते ॥
दैविकानां युगानान्तु सहस्रं परिसंख्यया ।
ब्राह्ममेकमहर्ज्ञेयं तावती रात्निरेव च ॥

[Four thousands of years, they say, is the Krita Yuga (Satya Yuga or the "Golden Age" of the world). Its morning twilight has just as many hundreds, and its period of evening dusk is of the same length (i.e., 400+4000+400=4800). In the other three ages, with their morning and evening twilights, the thousands and the hundreds decrease by one (i.e., 300+3000+300=3600; etc.). That fourfold cycle comprising 12,000 years is called an Age of the Gods. The sum of a thousand divine ages constitutes one day of Brahma; and of the same length is its night.]

The period of Satya Yuga is 4000 years in duration; 400 years before and after Satya Yuga proper are its *sandhis* or periods of mutation with the preceding and the succeeding Yugas respectively; hence 4800 years in all is the proper age of Satya Yuga. In the calculation of the period of other Yugas and Yugasandhis, it is laid down that the numeral one should be deducted from the numbers of both thousands and hundreds which indicate the periods of the previous Yugas and *sandhis.* From this rule it appears that 3000 years is the length of Treta Yuga, and 300 years before and after are its *sandhis,* the periods of mutation, which make a total of 3600 years.

So 2000 years is the age of Dwapara Yuga, with 200 years before and after as its *sandhis;* a total of 2400 years. Lastly, 1000 years is the length of Kali Yuga, with 100 years before and after as its *sandhis;* a total of 1200 years. Thus 12,000 years, the sum total of all periods of these four Yugas, is the length of one of the Daiva Yugas or Electric Couple, two of which, that is, 24,000 years, make the electric cycle complete.

From 11,501 B.C., when the Autumnal Equinox was on the first point of Aries, the sun began to move away from the point of its orbit nearest to the grand center toward the point farthest from it, and accordingly the intellectual power of man began to diminish. During the 4800 years which the sun took to pass through one of the Satya Couples or 4/20th part of its orbit, the intellect of man lost altogether the power of grasping spiritual knowledge. During the 3600 years following, which the sun took to pass through the Descending Treta Yuga, the intellect gradually lost all power of grasping the knowledge of divine magnetism. During the 2400 years next following, while the sun passed through the Descending Dwapara Yuga, the human intellect lost its power of grasping the knowledge of electricities and their attributes. In 1200 more years the sun passed through the Descending Kali Yuga and reached the point in its orbit which is farthest from the grand center; the Autumnal Equinox was on the first point of Libra. The intellectual power of man was so much diminished that it could no longer comprehend anything beyond the gross material of creation. The period around A.D. 500 was thus the darkest part of Kali Yuga and of the whole cycle of 24,000 years. History indeed bears out the accuracy of these ancient calculations of the Indian *rishis*, and records the widespread ignorance and suffering in all nations at that period.

From A.D. 499 onward, the sun began to advance toward the grand center, and the intellect of man started gradually to develop. During the 1100 years of the Ascending Kali Yuga, which brings us to A.D. 1599, the human intellect was so dense that it could not comprehend the electricities, *Sukshmabhuta,* the fine matters of creation. In the political world also, generally speaking, there was no peace in any kingdom.

Subsequent to this period, when the 100-year

transitional *sandhi* of Kali Yuga set in, to effect a union with the following Dwapara Yuga, men began to notice the existence of fine matters, *panchatanmatra* or the attributes of electricities; and political peace began to be established.

About A.D. 1600, William Gilbert discovered magnetic forces and observed the presence of electricity in all material substances. In 1609 Kepler discovered important laws of astronomy, and Galileo produced a telescope. In 1621 Drebbel of Holland invented the microscope. About 1670 Newton discovered the law of gravitation. In 1700 Thomas Savery made use of a steam engine in raising water. Twenty years later Stephen Gray discovered the action of electricity on the human body.

In the political world, people began to have respect for themselves, and civilization advanced in many ways. England united with Scotland and became a powerful kingdom. Napoleon Bonaparte introduced his new legal code into southern Europe. America won its independence, and many parts of Europe were peaceful.

With the advance of science, the world began to be covered with railways and telegraphic wires. By the help of steam engines, electric machines, and many other instruments, fine matters were brought into practical use, although their nature was not clearly understood. In 1899, on completion of the period of 200 years of Dwapara Sandhi, the time of mutation, the true Dwapara Yuga of 2000 years will commence and will give to mankind in general a thorough understanding of the electricities and their attributes.

Such is the great influence of Time which governs the universe. No man can overcome this influence except him who, blessed with pure love, the heavenly gift of nature, becomes divine; being baptized in the sacred stream *Pranava* (the holy *Aum* vibration), he comprehends the Kingdom of God.

The position of the world in the Dwapara Sandhi era at present (A.D. 1894) is not correctly shown in the Hindu almanacs. The astronomers and astrologers who calculate the almanacs have been guided by wrong annotations of certain Sanskrit scholars (such as Kulluka Bhatta) of the dark age of Kali Yuga, and now maintain that the length of Kali Yuga is 432,000 years, of which 4994 have (in A.D. 1894) passed away, leaving 427,006 years still remaining. A dark prospect! and fortunately one not true.

The mistake crept into almanacs for the first time during the reign of Raja Parikshit, just after the completion of the last Descending Dwapara Yuga. At that time Maharaja Yudhisthira, noticing the appearance of the dark Kali Yuga, made over his throne to his grandson, the said Raja Parikshit. Maharaja Yudhisthira, together with all the wise men of his court, retired to the Himalaya Mountains, the paradise of the world. Thus there was none in the court of Raja Parikshit who could understand the principle of correctly calculating the ages of the several Yugas.

Hence, after the completion of the 2400 years of the then current Dwapara Yuga, no one dared to make the introduction of the dark Kali Yuga more manifest by beginning to calculate from its first year and to put an end to the number of Dwapara years.

According to this wrong method of calculation, therefore, the first year of Kali Yuga was numbered 2401 along with the age of Dwapara Yuga. In A.D. 499, when 1200 years, the length of the true Kali Yuga, was complete, and the sun had reached the point of its orbit farthest from the grand center (when the Autumnal Equinox was on the first point of Libra in the heavens), the age of Kali in its darkest period was then numbered by 3600 years instead of by 1200.

With the commencement of the Ascending Kali Yuga, after A.D. 499, the sun began to advance in its orbit nearer to the grand center, and accordingly the intellectual power of man started to develop. Therefore the mistake in the almanacs began to be noticed by the wise men of the time, who found that the calculations of the ancient *rishis* had fixed the period of one Kali Yuga at 1200 years only. But as the intellect of these wise men was not yet suitably developed, they could make out only the mistake itself, and not the reason for it. By way of reconciliation, they fancied that 1200 years, the real age of Kali, were not the ordinary years of our earth, but were so many *daiva* years ("years of the gods"), consisting of 12 *daiva* months of 30 *daiva* days each, with each *daiva* day being equal to one ordinary solar year of our earth. Hence according to these men 1200 years of Kali Yuga must be equal to 432,000 years of our earth.

In coming to a right conclusion, however, we should take into consideration the position of the Vernal Equinox at spring in the year 1894.

The astronomical reference books show the Vernal Equinox now to be $20^0 54' 36''$ distant from the first point of Aries (the fixed star Revati), and by calculation it will appear that 1394 years have passed since the time when the Vernal Equinox began to recede from the first point of Aries.

Deducting 1200 years (the length of the last Ascending Kali Yuga) from 1394 years, we get 194 to indicate the present year of the world's entrance into the Ascending Dwapara Yuga. The mistake of older almanacs will thus be clearly explained when we add 3600 years to this period of 1394 years and get 4994 years — which according to the prevailing mistaken theory represents the present year (A.D. 1894) in the Hindu almanacs.

[Referring to the Diagram given in this book, the reader will see that the Autumnal Equinox is now (A.D. 1894) falling among the stars of the Virgo constellation, and in the Ascending Dwapara Yuga.]

In this book certain truths such as those about the properties of magnetism, its auras, different sorts of electricities, etc., have been mentioned, although modern science has not yet fully discovered them. The five sorts of electricity can be easily understood if one will direct his attention to the nerve properties, which are purely electrical in nature. Each of the five sensory nerves has its characteristic and unique function to perform. The optic nerve carries light and does not perform the functions of the auditory and other nerves; the auditory nerve in its turn carries sound only, without performing the functions of any other nerves, and so on. Thus it is clear that there are five sorts of electricity, corresponding to the five properties of cosmic electricity.

So far as magnetic properties are concerned, the grasping power of the human intellect is at present so limited that it would be quite useless to attempt to make the matter understood by the general public. The intellect of man in Treta Yuga will comprehend the attributes of divine magnetism (the next Treta Yuga will start in A.D. 4099). There are indeed exceptional personages now living who, having overcome the influence of Time, can grasp today what ordinary people cannot grasp; but this book is not for those exalted ones, who require nothing of it.

In concluding this introduction, we may observe that the different planets, exercising their influence over the various days of the week, have lent their names to their respective days; similarly, the different constellations of stars, having influence over various months, have lent their names to the Hindu months. Each of the great Yugas has much influence over the period of time covered by it; hence, in designating the years it is desirable that such terms should indicate to which Yuga they belong.

As the Yugas are calculated from the position of the equinox, the method of numbering the years in reference to their respective Yuga is based on a scientific principle; its use will obviate much inconvenience which has arisen in the past owing to association of the various eras with persons of eminence rather than with celestial phenomena of the fixed stars. We therefore propose to name and number the year in which this introduction has been written as 194 Dwapara, instead of A.D. 1894, to show the exact time of the Yuga now passing. This method of calculation was prevalent in India till the reign of Raja Vikramaditya, when the *Samvat* era was introduced. As the Yuga method of calculation recommends itself to reason, we follow it, and recommend that it be followed by the public in general.

Now, in this 194th year of Dwapara Yuga, the dark age of Kali having long since passed, the

world is reaching out for spiritual knowledge,
and men require loving help one from the other.
The publishing of this book, requested from me
by my holy *paramguru maharaj* Babaji, will, I hope,
be of spiritual service.

Swami Sri Yukteswar Giri

Serampore, West Bengal
The 26th Falgun, 194 Dwapara
(A.D. 1894)

कैवल्यदर्शनम्

CHAPTER 1

वेदः THE GOSPEL

SUTRA 1

नित्यं पूर्णमनाद्यनन्तं ब्रह्म परम् ।
तदेवैकमेवाद्वैतं सत् । १ ।

**Parambrahma (Spirit or God) is everlasting,
complete, without beginning or end. It is one, indi-
visible Being.***

The Eternal Father, God, *Swami Param-
brahma,* is the only Real Substance, *Sat,* and is all
in all in the universe.

Why God is not comprehensible. Man possesses
eternal faith and believes intuitively in the existence of a Substance, of which the objects of
sense—sound, touch, sight, taste, and smell, the
component parts of this visible world—are but
properties. As man identifies himself with his
material body, composed of the aforesaid properties, he is able to comprehend by these imperfect
organs these properties only, and not the Substance to which these properties belong. The Eter-

---

* Swami Sri Yukteswarji stated these *sutras* (precepts) in Sanskrit
only, as shown. The translation has been provided by Self-
Realization Fellowship. *(Publishers Note)*

nal Father, God, the only Substance in the universe, is therefore not comprehensible by man of
this material world, unless he becomes divine by
lifting his self above this creation of Darkness or
Maya. See Hebrews 11:1 and John 8:28.

> *"Now faith is the substance of things hoped for, the
> evidence of things not seen."*

> *"Then said Jesus unto them, When ye have lifted
> up the son of man, then shall ye know that I am he."*

SUTRA 2

तत्र सर्व्वज्ञप्रेमबीजञ्चित् सर्व्वशक्तिबीजमानन्दश्च ॥ २ ॥

**In It (Parambrahma) is the origin of all knowl-
edge and love, the root of all power and joy.**

***Prakriti* or Nature of God.** The Almighty Force,
Shakti, or in other words the Eternal Joy, *Ananda,*
which produces the world; and the Omniscient
Feeling, *Chit,* which makes this world conscious,
demonstrate the Nature, *Prakriti,* of God the
Father.

How God is comprehended. As man is the likeness of God, directing his attention inward he can
comprehend within him the said Force and Feeling, the sole properties of his Self—the Force
Almighty as his will, *Vasana,* with enjoyment,
Bhoga; and the Feeling Omniscient as his Con-

sciousness, *Chetana,* that enjoys, *Bhokta.* See Genesis 1:27.

> *"So God created man in his own image, in the image of God created he him; male and female created he them."*

SUTRA 3

तत्सर्व्वशक्तिवीजजड प्रकृतिवासनाया व्यक्तभावः ।
प्रणवशब्दः दिक्कालाणवोऽपि तस्य रूपाणि ॥ ३ ॥

Parambrahma causes creation, inert Nature (*Prakriti*), to emerge. From *Aum* (*Pranava*, the Word, the manifestation of the Omnipotent Force), come *Kala*, Time; *Desa*, Space; and *Anu*, the Atom (the vibratory structure of creation).

The Word, *Amen* (*Aum*), is the beginning of the Creation. The manifestation of Omnipotent Force (the Repulsion and its complementary expression, Omniscient Feeling or Love, the Attraction) is vibration, which appears as a peculiar sound: the Word, *Amen, Aum.* In its different aspects *Aum* presents the idea of change, which is Time, *Kala,* in the Ever-Unchangeable; and the idea of division, which is Space, *Desa,* in the Ever-Indivisible.

The Four Ideas: the Word, Time, Space, and the Atom. The ensuing effect is the idea of particles

—the innumerable atoms, *patra* or *anu*. These four—the Word, Time, Space, and the Atom— are therefore one and the same, and substantially nothing but mere ideas.

This manifestation of the Word (becoming flesh, the external material) created this visible world. So the Word, *Amen, Aum,* being the manifestation of the Eternal Nature of the Almighty Father or His Own Self, is inseparable from and nothing but God Himself; as the burning power is inseparable from and nothing but the fire itself. See Revelation 3:14; John 1:1,3,14.

> *"These things saith the Amen, the faithful and true witness, the beginning of the creation of God."*

> *"In the beginning was the Word, and the Word was with God, and the Word was God.... All things were made by him; and without him was not anything made that was made.... And the Word was made flesh and dwelt among us."*

SUTRA 4

तदेव जगत्कारणं माया ईश्वरस्य, तस्य व्यष्टिरविद्या ॥ ४ ॥

The cause of creation is *Anu* or the Atoms. En masse they are called *Maya* or the Lord's illusory power; each individual *Anu* is called *Avidya*, Ignorance.

Atoms the throne of Spirit the Creator. These

Atoms, which represent within and without the four ideas mentioned above, are the throne of Spirit, the Creator, which shining on them creates this universe. They are called en masse *Maya,* the Darkness, as they keep the Spiritual Light out of comprehension; and each of them separately is called *Avidya,* the Ignorance, as it makes man ignorant even of his own Self. Hence the aforesaid four ideas which give rise to all those confusions are mentioned in the Bible as so many beasts. Man, so long as he identifies himself with his gross material body, holds a position far inferior to that of the primal fourfold Atom and necessarily fails to comprehend the same. But when he raises himself to the level thereof, he not only comprehends this Atom, both inside and outside, but also the whole creation, both unmanifested and manifested (i.e., "before and behind"). See Revelation 4:6.

> *"And in the midst of the throne, and round about the throne, were four beasts full of eyes before and behind."*

SUTRA 5

तत्सर्व्वज्ञप्रेमबीजं परं तदेव कूटस्थचैतन्यम् ।
पुरुषोत्तमः तस्याभासः पुरुषः तस्मादभेदः । ५ ।

The Omniscient Love aspect of Parambrahma is *Kutastha Chaitanya.* **The individual Self, being Its manifestation, is one with It.**

Kutastha Chaitanya,* the Holy Ghost, *Purushot-tama. The manifestation of *Premabijam Chit* (Attraction, the Omniscient Love) is Life, the Omnipresent Holy Spirit, and is called the Holy Ghost, *Kutastha Chaitanya* or *Purushottama,* which shines on the Darkness, *Maya,* to attract every portion of it toward Divinity. But the Darkness, *Maya,* or its individual parts,* *Avidya* the Ignorance, being repulsion itself, cannot receive or comprehend the Spiritual Light, but reflects it.

Abhasa Chaitanya* or *Purusha,* the Sons of God. This Holy Ghost, being the manifestation of the Omniscient Nature of the Eternal Father, God, is no other substance than God Himself; and so these reflections of spiritual rays are called the Sons of God—*Abhasa Chaitanya* or *Purusha.* See John 1:4, 5, 11.

> *"In him was life; and the life was the light of men.*
>
> *"And the light shineth in darkness; and the darkness comprehended it not."*
>
> *"He came unto his own, and his own received him not."*

SUTRA 6

चित्सकाशादणोर्महत्त्वं तच्चित्त्वम्, तत्रसदध्यवसायः ।
सत्त्वं बुद्धिः ततस्तद्विपरीतं मनः
चरमंऽभिमानोऽहंकारस्तदेव जीवः । ६ ।

---

* That is, its presence in each man.

The Atom, under the influence of *Chit* (universal knowledge) forms the *Chitta* or the calm state of mind, which when spiritualized is called *Buddhi*, Intelligence. Its opposite is *Manas*, Mind, in which lives the *Jiva:* the self with *Ahamkara*, Ego, the idea of separate existence.

***Chitta,* the Heart; *Ahamkara,* Ego, the son of man.** This Atom, *Avidya,* the Ignorance, being under the influence of Universal Love, *Chit,* the Holy Spirit, becomes spiritualized, like iron filings in a magnetic aura, and possessed of consciousness, the power of feeling, when it is called *Mahat,* the Heart, *Chitta;* and being such, the idea of separate existence of self appears in it, which is called *Ahamkara,* Ego, the son of man.

***Buddhi,* the Intelligence; *Manas,* the Mind.** Being thus magnetized, it has two poles, one of which attracts it toward the Real Substance, *Sat,* and the other repels it from the same. The former is called *Sattva* or *Buddhi,* the Intelligence, which determines what is Truth; and the latter, being a particle of Repulsion, the Almighty Force spiritualized as aforesaid, produces the ideal world for enjoyment *(ananda)* and is called *Anandatwa* or *Manas,* the Mind.

SUTRA 7–10

तदहंकारचित्तविकारपञ्चतत्त्वानि । ७ ।
तान्येव कारणशरीरं पुरुषस्य । ८ ।

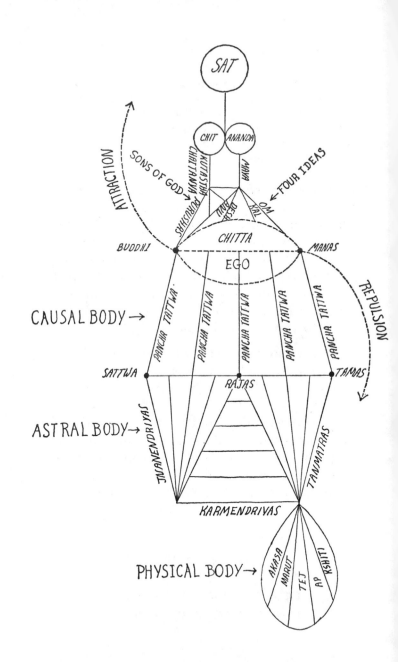

तेषां त्रिगुणेभ्यः पञ्चदश विषयेन्द्रियाणि । ६ ।
एतानि मनोबुद्धिभ्यां सह सप्तदशसूक्ष्माङ्गानि ।
लिङ्गशरीरस्य । १० ।

Chitta, the spiritualized Atom, in which *Aham-kara* (the idea of separate existence of Self) appears, has five manifestations (aura electricities).

They (the five aura electricities) constitute the causal body of *Purusha*.

The five electricities, *Pancha Tattwa*, from their three attributes, *Gunas — Sattva* (positive), *Rajas* (neutralizing), and *Tamas* (negative)—produce *Jnanendriyas* (organs of sense), *Karmendriyas* (organs of action), and *Tanmatras* (objects of sense).

These fifteen attributes plus Mind and Intelligence constitute the seventeen "fine limbs" of the subtle body, the *Lingasarira*.

Pancha Tattwa, **the Root-Causes of creation, are the causal body.** This spiritualized Atom, *Chitta* (the Heart), being the Repulsion manifested, produces five sorts of aura electricities from its five different parts: one from the middle, two from the two extremities, and the other two from the spaces intervening between the middle and each of the extremities. These five sorts of electricities, being attracted under the influence of Universal Love (the Holy Ghost) toward the Real Substance, *Sat*, pro-

OPPOSITE PAGE: This diagram, prepared by the publishers, is intended only to show the progression of development of various aspects of creation, and does not purport to illustrate their spatial relationship to one another.

duce a magnetic field which is called the body of
Sattva Buddhi, the Intelligence. These five electricities being the causes of all other creations are
called *Pancha Tattwa,* the five Root-Causes, and are
considered the causal body of *Purusha,* the Son of
God.

Three *Gunas*, the electric attributes. The electricities, being evolved from the polarized *Chitta,*
are also in a polarized state and are endowed with
its three attributes or *Gunas: Sattva* the positive,
Tamas the negative, and *Rajas* the neutralizing.

***Jnanendriyas*, the five organs of the senses.** The
positive attributes of the five electricities are *Jnanendriyas,* the organs of the senses—smell, taste,
sight, touch, and hearing—and being attracted
under the influence of *Manas,* Mind, the opposite
pole of this spiritualized Atom, constitute a body
of the same.

***Karmendriyas*, the five organs of action.** The
neutralizing attributes of the five electricities are
Karmendriyas, the organs of action—excretion,
generation, motion (feet), manual skill (hands),
and speech. These organs, being the manifestation of the neutralizing energy of the spiritualized
Atom, *Chitta* (the Heart), constitute an energetic
body, called the body of energy, the life force or
Prana.

***Vishaya* or *Tanmatras*, the five objects of the
senses.** The negative attributes of the five electricities are the five *Tanmatras* or objects of the

senses of smell, taste, sight, touch, and sound, which, being united with the organs of sense through the neutralizing power of the organs of action, satisfy the desires of the heart.

Lingasarira, the fine material body. These fifteen attributes with two poles—Mind and Intelligence—of the spiritualized Atom constitute *Lingasarira* or *Sukshmasarira,* the fine material body of *Purusha,* the Son of God.

SUTRAS 11, 12

ततः पञ्चतत्त्वानां स्थितिशीलतामसिकविषयपञ्चतन्मात्राणां
पञ्चीकरणेन स्थूलशरीरस्याङ्गानि जडीभूतपञ्चक्षित्यप्तेजो
    मरुद्व्योमान्युद्भूतानि । ११ ।
एतान्येव चतुर्विंशतिः तत्त्वानि । १२ ।

The aforesaid five objects, which are the negative attributes of the five electricities, being combined produce the idea of gross matter in its five forms: *Kshiti*, solids; *Ap*, liquids; *Tejas*, fire; *Marut*, gaseous substances; and *Akasha*, ether.

These five forms of gross matter and the aforesaid fifteen attributes, together with *Manas*, Mind, sense consciousness; *Buddhi*, discriminative Intelligence; *Chitta*, the Heart or power of feeling; and *Ahamkara*, the Ego, constitute the twenty-four basic principles of creation.

Gross material body. The aforesaid five objects, which are the negative attributes of the five electricities, being combined together produce the idea of gross matter which appears to us in five different varieties: *Kshiti*, the solid; *Ap*, the liquid; *Tejas*, the fiery; *Marut*, the gaseous; and *Vyoma* or *Akasha*, the ethereal. These constitute the outer covering called *Sthulasarira*, the gross material body of *Purusha*, the Son of God.

Twenty-four Elders. These five gross matters and the aforesaid fifteen attributes together with *Manas*, the Mind; *Buddhi*, the Intelligence; *Chitta*, the Heart; and *Ahamkara*, the Ego, constitute the twenty-four principles or Elders, as mentioned in the Bible. See Revelation 4:4.

> *"And round about the throne were four and twenty seats; and upon the seats I saw four and twenty elders."*

The aforesaid twenty-four principles, which completed the creation of Darkness, *Maya*, are nothing more than the development of Ignorance, *Avidya;* and as this Ignorance is composed only of ideas as mentioned above, creation has in reality no substantial existence, but is a mere play of ideas on the Eternal Substance, God the Father.

SUTRA 13

तत्रैव चतुर्दशभुवनानि व्याख्यातानि । १३ ।

This universe is differentiated into fourteen spheres, seven *Swargas* and seven *Patalas*.

Seven Spheres or *Swargas*. This universe thus described, commencing from the Eternal Substance, God, down to the gross material creation, has been distinguished into seven different spheres, *Swargas* or *Lokas*.

7th Sphere, *Satyaloka*. The foremost of these is *Satyaloka,* the sphere of God—the only Real Substance, *Sat,* in the universe. No name can describe it, nor can anything in the creation of Darkness or Light designate it. This sphere is therefore called *Anama,* the Nameless.

6th Sphere, *Tapoloka*. The next in order is *Tapoloka,* the sphere of the Holy Spirit which is the Eternal Patience, as it remains forever undisturbed by any limited idea. Because it is not approachable even by the Sons of God as such, it is called *Agama,* the Inaccessible.

5th Sphere, *Janaloka*. Next is *Janaloka,* the sphere of spiritual reflection, the Sons of God, wherein the idea of separate existence of Self originates. As this sphere is above the comprehension of anyone in the creation of Darkness, *Maya,* it is called *Alakshya,* the Incomprehensible.

4th Sphere, *Maharloka*. Then comes *Maharloka,* the sphere of the Atom, the beginning of the creation of Darkness, *Maya,* upon which the Spirit is reflected. This, the connecting link, is the only way between the spiritual and the material creation and is called the Door, *Dasamadwara.*

3rd Sphere, *Swarloka*. Around this Atom is *Swarloka,* the sphere of magnetic aura, the electricities. This sphere, being characterized by the absence of all the creation (even the organs and their objects, the fine material things), is called *Mahasunya,* the Great Vacuum.

2nd Sphere, *Bhuvarloka*. The next is *Bhuvarloka,* the sphere of electric attributes. As the gross matters of the creation are entirely absent from this sphere, and it is conspicuous by the presence of the fine matters only, it is called *Sunya,* the Vacuum Ordinary.

1st Sphere, *Bhuloka*. The last and lowest sphere is *Bhuloka,* the sphere of gross material creation, which is always visible to everyone.

***Sapta Patalas,* seven churches.** As God created man in His own image, so is the body of man like unto the image of this universe. The material body of man has also seven vital places within it called *Patalas.* Man, turning toward his Self and advancing in the right way, perceives the Spiritual Light in these places, which are described in the Bible as so many churches; the lights like stars perceived therein are as so many angels. See Revelation 1:12, 13, 16, 20.

> *"And being turned, I saw seven golden candlesticks, and in the midst of the seven candlesticks one like unto the son of man...."*

> *"And he had in his right hand seven stars...."*

> *"The seven stars are the angels of the seven*

churches; and the seven candlesticks which thou sawest are the seven churches."

14 *Bhuvanas*, the stages of creation. The above-mentioned seven spheres or *Swargas* and the seven *Patalas* constitute the fourteen *Bhuvanas,* the fourteen distinguishable stages of the creation.

SUTRA 14

त एव पञ्च कोषाः पुरुषस्य । १४ ।

Purusha is covered by five *koshas* or sheaths.

5 *Koshas* or Sheaths. This *Purusha,* the Son of God is screened by five coverings called the *koshas* or sheaths.

Heart, the 1st *Kosha*. The first of these five is Heart, *Chitta,* the Atom, composed of four ideas as mentioned before, which feels or enjoys, and thus being the seat of bliss, *ananda,* is called *Anandamaya Kosha.*

Buddhi, the 2nd *Kosha*. The second is the magnetic-aura electricities, manifestations of *Buddhi,* the Intelligence that determines what is truth. Thus, being the seat of knowledge, *jnana,* it is called *Jnanamaya Kosha.*

Manas, the 3rd *Kosha*. The third is the body of *Manas,* the Mind, composed of the organs of senses, as mentioned above, and called the *Man-omaya Kosha*.

Prana, the 4th *Kosha*. The fourth is the body of energy, life force or *Prana,* composed of the organs of action as described before, and thus called *Pranamaya Kosha.*

Gross matter, the 5th *Kosha*. The fifth and last of these sheaths is the gross matter, the Atom's outer coating, which, becoming *Anna,* nourishment, supports this visible world and thus is called the *Annamaya Kosha.*

Action of Love. The action of Repulsion, the manifestation of the Omnipotent Energy, being thus completed, the action of Attraction (the Omnipotent Love in the core of the heart) begins to be manifested. Under the influence of this Omniscient Love, the Attraction, the Atoms, being attracted toward one another, come nearer and nearer, taking ethereal, gaseous, fiery, liquid, and solid forms.

Inanimate kingdom. Thus this visible world becomes adorned with suns, planets, and moons, which we call the inanimate kingdom of the creation.

Vegetable kingdom. In this manner, when the action of Divine Love becomes well developed, the evolution of *Avidya,* Ignorance (the particle of Darkness, *Maya,* the Omnipotent Energy manifested), begins to be withdrawn. *Annamaya Kosha,* the Atom's outer coating of gross matter being thus withdrawn, *Pranamaya Kosha* (the sheath composed of *Karmendriyas,* the organs of action) begins to operate. In this organic state the Atoms, embracing each other more closely to their heart, appear as the vegetable kingdom in the creation.

Animal kingdom. When the *Pranamaya Kosha* becomes withdrawn, the *Manomaya Kosha* (the sheath composed of *Jnanendriyas,* the organs of sense) comes to light. The Atoms then perceive the nature of the external world and, attracting other Atoms of different nature, form bodies as necessary for enjoyment, and thus the animal kingdom appears in the creation.

Mankind. When *Manomaya Kosha* becomes withdrawn, *Jnanamaya Kosha* (the body of Intelligence composed of electricities) becomes perceptible. The Atom, acquiring the power of determining right and wrong, becomes man, the rational being in the creation.

***Devata* or Angel.** When man, cultivating the Divine Spirit or Omniscient Love within his heart, is able to withdraw this *Jnanamaya Kosha,* then the innermost sheath, *Chitta,* the Heart (composed of four ideas), becomes manifest. Man is then called *Devata* or Angel in the creation.

Free, *Sannyasi.* When the Heart or innermost sheath is also withdrawn, there is no longer anything to keep man in bondage to this creation of Darkness, *Maya.* He then becomes free, *Sannyasi,*

the Son of God, and enters into the creation of
Light.

SUTRAS 15, 16

स्थूलज्ञानक्रमात् सूक्ष्मविषयेन्द्रियज्ञानं स्वप्नवत् । १५ ।
तत्क्रमात् मनोबुद्धिज्ञानञ्चायातमिति परोक्षम् । १६ ।

**Just as the objects seen in our dreams are found,
when we awake, to be insubstantial, so our waking
perceptions are likewise unreal—a matter of inference only.**

Sleeping and waking states. When man compares his ideas relating to gross matters conceived
in the wakeful state with his conception of ideas in
dream, the similarity existing between them naturally leads him to conclude that this external
world also is not what it appears to be.

When he looks for further explanation, he
finds that all his wakeful conceptions are substantially nothing but mere ideas caused by the union
of five objects of sense (the negative attributes of
the five internal electricities) with the five organs
of sense (their positive attributes) through the
medium of five organs of action (the neutralizing
attributes of the electricities).

This union is effected by the operation of
Mind (*Manas*) and conceived or grasped by the
Intelligence (*Buddhi*). Thus it is clear that all con-

ceptions which man forms in his wakeful state are mere inferential *Parokshajnana*—a matter of inference only.

SUTRA 17

ततः सद्गुरुलाभो भक्तियोगश्च तेनापरोक्षः । १७ ।

What is needed is a Guru, a Savior, who will awaken us to *Bhakti* (devotion) and to perceptions of Truth.

When man finds his *Sat-Guru* or Savior. In this way, when man understands by his *Parokshajnana* (correct inference) the nothingness of the external world, he appreciates the position of John the Baptist, the divine personage who witnessed Light and bore testimony of Christ, after his heart's love, the heavenly gift of Nature, had become developed.

Any advanced sincere seeker may be fortunate in having the Godlike company of some one of such personages, who may kindly stand to him as his Spiritual Preceptor, *Sat-Guru,* the Savior. Following affectionately the holy precepts of these divine personages, man becomes able to direct all his organs of sense inward to their common center—the sensorium, *Trikuti* or *Sushumnadwara,* the door of the interior world—where he comprehends the Voice, like a peculiar "knocking" sound, [the Cosmic Vibration that is] the Word, *Amen, Aum;* and sees the God-sent luminous body of *Radha,* symbolized in the Bible as the Forerunner or John the Baptist. See Revelation 3:14,20 and John 1:6,8,23.

> *"These things saith the Amen, the faithful and true witness, the beginning of the creation of God....Behold, I stand at the door, and knock; if any man hear my voice and open the door, I will come in to him and will sup with him, and he with me."*

> *"There was a man sent from God, whose name was John .... He was not that Light, but was sent to bear witness of that Light....He said, I am the voice of one crying in the wilderness, Make straight the way of the Lord."*

Ganga, Yamuna, or Jordan, the holy streams. From the peculiar nature of this sound, issuing as it does like a stream from a higher unknown region and losing itself in the gross material creation, it is figuratively designated by various sects of people by the names of different rivers that they consider as sacred; for example, Ganga by the Hindus, Yamuna by the Vaishnavas,* and Jordan† by the Christians.

The 2nd birth. Through his luminous body, man, believing in the existence of the true Light—the Life of this universe—becomes baptized or ab-

* Worshipers of Vishnu, God as Preserver.
† Matthew 3:13–17.

sorbed in the holy stream of the sound. The baptism is, so to speak, the second birth of man and is called *Bhakti Yoga,** without which man can never comprehend the real internal world, the kingdom of God. See John 1:9 and 3:3.

"That was the true Light, which lighteth every man that cometh into the world."

"Verily, verily, I say unto thee, Except a man be born again, he cannot see the kingdom of God."

***Aparokshajnana*, the real comprehension.** In this state the son of man begins to repent and, turning back from the gross material creation, creeps toward his Divinity, the Eternal Substance, God. When the developments of ignorance are stopped, man gradually comprehends the true character of this creation of Darkness, *Maya,* as a mere play of ideas of the Supreme Nature on His own Self, the only Real Substance. This true comprehension is called *Aparokshajnana.*

SUTRA 18

यदात्मनः परमात्मनि दर्शनन्ततः कैवल्यम् । १८ ।

Emancipation (*Kaivalya*) is obtained when one realizes the oneness of his Self with the Universal Self, the Supreme Reality.

* Union with God through Love, the Attraction, which is constantly drawing man toward the kingdom of God. *(Publisher's Note)*

***Sannyasi* or Christ the anointed Savior.** When all
the developments of Ignorance are withdrawn,
the heart, being perfectly clear and purified, no
longer merely reflects the Spiritual Light but actively manifests the same, and thus being consecrated and anointed, man becomes *Sannyasi,* free,
or Christ the Savior.* See John 1:33.

> *"Upon whom thou shalt see the Spirit descending,
> and remaining on him, the same is he which baptizeth
> with the Holy Ghost."*

Baptized in the stream of Light. Through this
Savior the son of man becomes again baptized or
absorbed in the stream of Spiritual Light, and,
rising above the creation of Darkness, *Maya,* enters into the spiritual world and becomes unified
with *Abhasa Chaitanya* or *Purusha,* the Son of God,
as was the case with Lord Jesus of Nazareth. In
this state man is saved for ever and ever from the
bondage of Darkness, *Maya.* See John 1:12 and
3:5.

> *"But as many as received him, to them gave he
> power to become the Sons of God, even to them that
> believe on his name."*

> *"Verily, verily, I say unto thee, except a man be
> born of water and of the Spirit, he cannot enter into the
> kingdom of God."*

* That is, he becomes one with Christ Consciousness, the reflected
consciousness of the Eternal Father God in creation, immanent in
the Word or *Aum,* the Cosmic Vibration. Thus is he freed or saved
from the darkness of *Maya,* the delusion of separateness from the
Father. *(Publisher's Note)*

Sacrifice of self. When man thus entering into the spiritual world becomes a Son of God, he comprehends the universal Light—the Holy Ghost —as a perfect whole, and his Self as nothing but a mere idea resting on a fragment of the *Aum* Light. Then he sacrifices himself to the Holy Ghost, the altar of God; that is, abandons the vain idea of his separate existence, and becomes one integral whole.

Kaivalya, **the unification.** Thus, being one with the universal Holy Spirit of God the Father, he becomes unified with the Real Substance, God. This unification of Self with the Eternal Substance, God, is called *Kaivalya.** See Revelation 3:21.

> *"To him that overcometh will I grant to sit with me in my throne, even as I also overcame, and am set down with my Father in his throne."*

* Literally, "isolation," absolute independence or emancipation through oneness with God. *(Publisher's Note)*

CHAPTER 2

अभीष्टम् । THE GOAL

SUTRA 1

अतां मुक्तिजिज्ञासा । १ ।

Hence there is desire for emancipation.

Liberation, the prime object. When man understands even by way of inference the true nature of
this creation, the true relation existing between
this creation and himself; and when he further
understands that he is completely blinded by the
influence of Darkness, *Maya,* and that it is the
bondage of Darkness alone which makes him
forget his real Self and brings about all his sufferings, he naturally wishes to be relieved from all
these evils. This relief from evil, or liberation
from the bondage of *Maya,* becomes the prime
object of his life.

SUTRA 2

मुक्तिः स्वरूपेऽवस्थानम् । २ ।

**Liberation is stabilization of *Purusha* (*jiva*, soul)
in its real Self.**

Residing in Self is liberation. When man raises himself above the idea creation of this Darkness, *Maya,* and passes completely out of its influence, he becomes liberated from bondage and is placed in his real Self, the Eternal Spirit.

SUTRA 3

तदा सर्वक्लेशनिवृत्तिः परमार्थसिद्धिश्च । ३ ।

Then there is cessation of all pain and the attainment of the ultimate aim (true fulfillment, God-realization).

Liberation is salvation. On attaining this liberation, man becomes saved from all his troubles, and all the desires of his heart are fulfilled, so the ultimate aim of his life is accomplished.

SUTRA 4

इतरत्र अपूर्णकामजन्मजन्मान्तरव्यापि दुःखम् । ४ ।

Otherwise, birth after birth, man experiences the misery of unfulfilled desires.

Why man suffers. So long, however, as man identifies himself with his material body and fails to find repose in his true Self, he feels his wants according as his heart's desires remain unsatisfied. To satisfy them he has to appear often in flesh and blood on the stage of life, subject to the influence of Darkness, *Maya,* and has to suffer all the troubles of life and death not only in the present but in the future as well.

SUTRAS 5, 6

क्लेशोऽविद्यामातृकः । ५ ।

भावेऽभावोऽभावे भाव इत्येवं बोधोऽविद्या । ६ ।

Troubles are born from *Avidya,* Ignorance. Ignorance is the perception of the nonexistent, and the nonperception of the Existent.

What is ignorance? Ignorance, *Avidya,* is misconception, or is the erroneous conception of the existence of that which does not exist. Through *Avidya* man believes that this material creation is the only thing that substantially exists, there being nothing beyond, forgetting that this material creation is substantially nothing and is a mere play of ideas on the Eternal Spirit, the only Real Substance, beyond the comprehension of the material creation. This Ignorance is not only a trouble in itself but is also the source of all the other troubles of man.

SUTRAS 7-12

तदेवावरणविक्षेपशक्ति विशिष्टत्वात्

क्षेत्रमस्मिताभिनिवेशरागद्वेषाणाम् । ७ ।

तस्यावरणशक्तेरस्मिताभिनिवेशौ विक्षेपशक्तेश्च रागद्वेषौ ।८ ।
स्वामिशक्त्योर्विविक्तज्ञानमस्मिता । ९ ।
प्राकृतिकसंस्कारमात्रमभिनिवेशः । १० ।
सुखकरविषयतृष्णा रागः । ११ ।
दुःखकरविषयत्यागतृष्णा द्वेषः । १२ ।

Avidya, Ignorance, having the twofold power of
polarity, manifests as egoism, attachment, aversion,
and (blind) tenacity.

The darkening power of *Maya* produces egoism
and (blind) tenacity; the polarity power of *Maya*
produces attachment (attraction) and aversion
(repulsion).

Egoism results from a lack of discrimination
between the physical body and the real Self.

Tenacity is a result of natural conditioning (belief in Nature and her laws as final, instead of belief
in the all-causative powers of the Soul).

Attachment means thirst for the objects of happiness.

Aversion means desire for the removal of the
objects of unhappiness.

Ignorance is the source of all troubles. In order
to understand how this Ignorance is the source of
all other troubles we should remember (as has
been explained in the previous chapter) that Ignorance, *Avidya,* is nothing but a particle of
Darkness, *Maya,* taken distributively, and as such
it possesses the two properties of *Maya.* The one
is its darkening power, by the influence of which

man is prevented from grasping anything beyond the material creation. This darkening power produces *Asmita* or Egoism, the identification of Self with the material body, which is but the development of Atom, the particles of the universal force; and *Abhinivesa* or blind tenacity to the belief in the validity and ultimate worth of the material creation.

By virtue of the second of the properties of *Maya,* Ignorance or *Avidya* in its polarized state produces attraction for certain objects and repulsion for others. The objects so attracted are the objects of pleasure, for which an Attachment, *Raga,* is formed. The objects that are repulsed are the objects producing pain, for which an Aversion, *Dwesha,* is formed.

SUTRA 13

क्लेशमूलं कर्म्म तद्विपाक एव दुःखम् । १३ ।

The root of pain is egoistic actions, which (being based on delusions) lead to misery.

Why man is bound. By the influence of these five troubles—Ignorance, Egoism, Attachment, Aversion, and Tenacity to the material creation—man is induced to involve himself in egoistic works and in consequence he suffers.

SUTRAS 14, 15

सर्वदुःखानां निवृत्तिरित्यर्थः । १४ ।
निवृत्तावप्यनुवृत्त्यभावः परमः । १५ ।

Man's purpose is complete freedom from un-happiness.

Once he has banished all pain beyond possibility of return, he has attained the highest goal.

Ultimate aim of the heart. With man the cessation of all suffering is *Artha,* the heart's immediate aim. The complete extirpation of all these sufferings so that their recurrence becomes impossible, is *Paramartha,* the ultimate goal.

SUTRAS 16–21

सर्वकामपूर्णत्वे सर्वदुःखमूलक्लेशनिवृत्तिः तदा
    परमार्थसिद्धिः । १६ ।
सच्चिदानन्दमयत्वप्राप्तिरिति स्थिरकामाः । १७ ।
सद्गुरुदत्तसाधनप्रभावात् चित्तस्य प्रसाद एवानन्दः । १८ ।
ततः सर्वदुःखानां हानन्तादा सर्वभावोदयश्चित् । १६ ।
तत आत्मनो नित्यत्वोपलब्धिः सत् । २० ।
तदेव स्वरूपं पुरुषस्य । २१ ।

Existence, consciousness, and bliss are the three longings (of the human heart).

Ananda,* bliss, is the contentment of heart attained by the ways and means suggested by the Savior, the *Sat-Guru.

> *Chit*, true consciousness, brings about the complete destruction of all troubles and the rise of all virtues.
>
> *Sat*, existence, is attained by realization of the permanency of the soul.
>
> These three qualities constitute the real nature of man.
>
> All desires being fulfilled, and all miseries removed, the achievement of *Paramartha* (the highest goal) is made.

The real necessities. Man naturally feels great necessity for *Sat*, Existence; *Chit*, Consciousness; and *Ananda*, Bliss. These three are the real necessities of the human heart and have nothing to do with anything outside his Self. They are essential properties of his own nature, as explained in the previous chapter.

How man attains Bliss. When man becomes fortunate in securing the favor of any divine personage, *Sat-Guru* (the Savior), and affectionately following his holy precepts is able to direct all his attention inward, he becomes capable of satisfying all the wants of his heart and can thereby gain contentment, *Ananda*, the Real Bliss.

How Consciousness appears. With his heart thus contented, man becomes able to fix his attention upon anything he chooses and can comprehend all its aspects. So *Chit*, Consciousness of all the modifications of Nature up to its first and primal manifestation, the Word (Amen, *Aum*),

and even of his own Real Self, gradually appears.
And being absorbed in the stream thereof, man
becomes baptized and begins to repent and return toward his Divinity, the Eternal Father,
whence he had fallen. See Revelation 2:5.

*"Remember therefore from whence thou art fallen,
and repent."*

How Existence is realized. Man, being conscious of his own real position and of the nature
of this creation of Darkness, *Maya,* becomes possessed of absolute power over it, and gradually
withdraws all the developments of Ignorance. In
this way, freed from the control of this creation of
Darkness, he comprehends his own Self as Inde-
structible and Ever-Existing Real Substance. So
Sat, the Existence of Self, comes to light.

How main object of the heart is attained. All the
necessities of the heart—*Sat,* Existence; *Chit,*
Consciousness; and *Ananda,* Bliss—having been
attained, Ignorance, the mother of evils, becomes
emaciated and consequently all troubles of this
material world, which are the sources of all sorts
of sufferings, cease forever. Thus the ultimate
aim of the heart is effected.

SUTRA 22

तदा सर्वकामपूर्णापरमार्थसिद्धिकात् गुणानाम्प्रतिप्रसव
आत्मनः स्वरूपप्रतिष्ठा, तदेव कैवल्यम् । २२ ।

All fulfillments of his nature attained, man is not merely a reflector of divine light but becomes actively united with Spirit. This state is *Kaivalya*, oneness.

How man finds salvation. In this state, all the necessities having been attained and the ultimate aim effected, the heart becomes perfectly purified and, instead of merely reflecting the spiritual light, actively manifests the same. Man, being thus consecrated or anointed by the Holy Spirit, becomes Christ, the anointed Savior. Entering the kingdom of Spiritual Light, he becomes the Son of God.

In this state man comprehends his Self as a fragment of the Universal Holy Spirit, and, abandoning the vain idea of his separate existence, unifies himself with the Eternal Spirit; that is, becomes one and the same with God the Father. This unification of Self with God is *Kaivalya,* which is the Ultimate Object of all created beings. See John 14:11.

"Believe me that I am in the Father, and the Father in me."

CHAPTER 3

साधनम् THE PROCEDURE

SUTRAS 1-4

तपःस्वाध्यायब्रह्मनिधानानि यज्ञः । १ ।

मात्रास्पर्शेषु तितिक्षा तपः । २ ।

आत्मतत्त्वोपदेशश्रवणमननिदिध्यासनमेव स्वाध्यायः । ३ ।

प्रणवशब्द एव पन्था ब्रह्मणः तस्मिन्

आत्मसमर्पणं ब्रह्मनिधानम् । ४ ।

Yajna, **sacrifice, means penance (***Tapas***), deep study (***Swadhyaya***), and the practice of meditation on *Aum* (***Brahmanidhana***).**

Penance is patience or even-mindedness in all conditions (equanimity amidst the essential dualities of *Maya;* cold and heat, pain and pleasure, etc.).

***Swadhyaya* consists of reading or hearing spiritual truth, pondering it, and forming a definite conception of it.**

(Meditation on) *Pranava*, the divine sound of *Aum*, is the only way to Brahman (Spirit), salvation.

Patience, faith, and holy work explained. *Tapas* is religious mortification or patience both in enjoyments and in sufferings. *Swadhyaya* is *sravana,* study, with *manana,* deep attention, and thereby *nididhyasana,* forming of an idea of the true faith about Self; that is, what I am, whence I came, where I shall go, what I have come for, and other

such matters concerning Self. *Brahmanidhana* is
the baptism or merging of Self in the stream of
the Holy Sound (*Pranava, Aum*), which is the holy
work performed to attain salvation and the only
way by which man can return to his Divinity, the
Eternal Father, whence he has fallen. See Revelation 2:19.

> *"I know thy works, and charity, and service, and
> faith, and thy patience, and thy works; and the last to be
> more than the first."*

SUTRAS 5, 6

श्रद्धावीर्य्यस्मृतिसमाध्यनुष्ठानात् तस्यािविर्भावः । ५ ।
स्वभावजप्रेम्णः वेगतीव्रता श्रद्धा । ६ ।

Aum **is heard through cultivation of** *Sraddha*
(heart's natural love), *Virya* **(moral courage),** *Smriti*
(memory of one's divinity), and *Samadhi* **(true
concentration).**

Sraddha **is intensification of the heart's natural
love.**

How the Holy Sound manifests. This Holy Sound
Pranava Sabda manifests spontaneously through
culture of *Sraddha,* the energetic tendency of the
heart's natural love; *Virya,* moral courage; *Smriti,*
true conception; and *Samadhi,* true concentration.

The virtue of Love. The heart's natural love is the
principal requisite to attain a holy life. When this

love, the heavenly gift of Nature, appears in the heart, it removes all causes of excitation from the system and cools it down to a perfectly normal state; and, invigorating the vital powers, expels all foreign matters—the germs of diseases—by natural ways (perspiration and so forth). It thereby makes man perfectly healthy in body and mind, and enables him to understand properly the guidance of Nature.

When this love becomes developed in man it makes him able to understand the real position of his own Self as well as of others surrounding him.

With the help of this developed love, man becomes fortunate in gaining the Godlike company of the divine personages and is saved forever. Without this love, man cannot live in the natural way, neither can he keep company with the fit person for his own welfare; he becomes often excited by the foreign matters taken into his system through mistakes in understanding the guidance of Nature, and in consequence he suffers in body and mind. He can never find any peace whatever, and his life becomes a burden. Hence the culture of this love, the heavenly gift, is the principal requisite for the attainment of holy salvation; it is impossible for man to advance a step toward the same without it. See Revelation 2:2–4.

"I know thy works, and thy labor, and thy patience,
and how thou canst not bear them which are evil: and

thou hast tried them which say they are apostles, and are not, and hast found them liars.

"And hast borne and hast patience, and for my name's sake hast labored, and hast not fainted.

"Nevertheless I have somewhat against thee, because thou hast left thy first love."

SUTRAS 7, 8

श्रद्धासेवितसद्गुरोः स्वभावजोपदेशपालने वीर्य्यलाभः । ७ ।
सर्व एव गुरवः सन्तापहारकाः संशयच्छेदकाः शान्तिप्रदायकाः
सत् तत्सङ्गः ब्रह्मवत् करणीयः, विपरीतमसत्
विषवद्वर्जनीयम् । ८ ।

Moral courage (*Virya*) arises from *Sraddha*, directing one's love toward the guru, and from affectionately following his instructions.

Those who remove our troubles, dispel our doubts, and bestow peace are true teachers. They perform a Godlike work. Their opposites (those who increase our doubts and difficulties) are harmful to us and should be avoided like poison.

As explained in the previous chapter, this creation is substantially nothing but a mere idea-play of Nature on the only Real Substance, God, the Eternal Father, who is Guru—the Supreme —in this universe. All things of this creation are therefore no other substance than this Guru, the Supreme Father, God Himself, perceived in plurality by the manifold aspects of the play of Nature. See John 10:34 and Psalm 82:6.

"Jesus answered them, Is it not written in your law, I said, Ye are gods?"

"I have said, Ye are gods; and all of you are children of the most High."

Out of this creation, the object that relieves us of our miseries and doubts and administers peace to us, whether animate or inanimate, and however insignificant the same may be, is entitled to our utmost respect. Even if it be regarded by others as an object of vilest contempt, it should be accepted as *Sat* (Savior) and its company as Godlike. That which produces opposite results, destroying our peace, throwing us into doubts, and creating our miseries, should be considered *Asat,* the bane of all good, and should be avoided as such. The Indian sages have a saying:

अप्सु देवो मनुष्याणां दिवि देवो मनीषिणाम् ।
काष्ठलोष्ट्रेषु मूर्खाणां युक्तस्यात्मनि देवता ॥

[Some consider the deities to exist in water (i.e., natural elements) while the learned consider them to exist in heaven (astral world); the unwise seek them in wood and stones (i.e., in images or symbols), but the Yogi realizes God in the sanctuary of his own Self.]

To attain salvation men choose as their Savior the objects that they can comprehend according to their own stage of evolution. Thus, in general, people think that illness is a dire calamity; and as water, when properly administered, tends to remove illness, ignorant men may choose for their Divinity water itself.

Philosophers, being able to comprehend the internal electrical Light that shines within them, find their heart's love flowing energetically toward the Light that relieves them of all causes of excitation, cools down their system to a normal state, and, invigorating their vital powers, makes them perfectly healthy, both in body and in mind. They then accept this Light as their Divinity or Savior.

Ignorant people in their blind faith would accept a piece of wood or stone as their Savior or Divinity in the external creation, for which their heart's natural love will develop till by its energetic tendency it will relieve them of all exciting causes, cool their system down to a normal state, and invigorate their vital powers. The adepts, on the other hand, having full control over the whole material world, find their Divinity or Savior in Self and not outside in the external world.

Regard the Guru with deep love. To keep company with the Guru is not only to be in his physical presence (as this is sometimes impossible), but mainly means to keep him in our hearts and to be one with him in principle and to attune ourselves with him.

This thought has been expressed by Lord

Bacon: "A crowd is not a company, it is a mere gallery of faces." To keep company, therefore, with the Godlike object is to associate him with *Sraddha,* the heart's love intensified in the sense above explained, by keeping his appearance and attributes fully in mind, and by reflecting on the same and affectionately following his instructions, lamblike. See John 1:29.

"Behold the Lamb of God, which taketh away the sin of the world."

By so doing, when man becomes able to conceive the sublime status of his divine brothers, he may be fortunate in remaining in their company and in securing help from any one of them whom he may choose as his Spiritual Preceptor, *Sat-Guru,* the Savior.

Thus, to resume, *Virya* or moral courage can be obtained by the culture of *Sraddha,* that is, by devoting one's natural love to his Preceptor, by being always in his company (in the internal sense already explained), and by following with affection his holy instructions as they are freely and spontaneously given.

SUTRAS 9-11

तद्वीर्यं यमनियमानुष्ठानत् दृढभूमिः । ९ ।
अहिंसासत्यास्तेयब्रह्मचर्यापरिग्रहाद्यो यमः । १० ।
शौचसन्तोषसद्गुरूपदेशपालनाद्यः नियमः । ११ ।

**Moral courage is strengthened by observance of
Yama (morality or self-control) and *Niyama* (religious rules).**

***Yama* comprises noninjury to others, truthful-
ness, nonstealing, continence, and noncovetousness.**

***Niyama* means purity of body and mind, con-
tentment in all circumstances, and obedience (following the instructions of the guru).**

Firmness of moral courage can be attained
by the culture of *Yama,* the religious forbearances:
abstention from cruelty, dishonesty, covetousness,
unnatural living, and unnecessary possessions;
and of *Niyama,* the religious observances: purity
in body and mind—cleaning the body externally
and internally from all foreign matters which,
being fermented, create different sorts of diseases
in the system, and clearing the mind from all
prejudices and dogmas that make one narrow—
contentment in all circumstances; and obedience
to the holy precepts of the divine personages.

What is natural living? To understand what natural living is, it will be necessary to distinguish it
from what is unnatural. Living depends upon the
selection of (1) food, (2) dwelling, and (3) company. To live naturally, the lower animals can
select these for themselves by the help of their
instincts and the natural sentinels placed at the
sensory entrances—the organs of sight, hearing,
touch, smell, and taste. With men in general,
however, these organs are so much perverted by

unnatural living from very infancy that little re-
liance can be placed on their judgments. To understand, therefore, what our natural needs are,
we ought to depend upon observation, experiment, and reason.

What is natural food for man? First, to select
our natural food, our observation should be directed to the formation of the organs that aid in
digestion and nutrition, the teeth and digestive
canal; to the natural tendency of the organs of
sense which guide animals to their food; and to
the nourishment of the young.

Observation of teeth. By observation of the
teeth we find that in carnivorous animals the incisors are little developed, but the canines are of
striking length, smooth and pointed, to seize the
prey. The molars also are pointed; these points,
however, do not meet, but fit closely side by side
to separate the muscular fibers.

In the herbivorous animals the incisors are
strikingly developed, the canines are stunted
(though occasionally developed into weapons, as
in elephants), the molars are broad-topped and
furnished with enamel on the sides only.

In the frugivorous all the teeth are of nearly
the same height; the canines are little projected,
conical, and blunt (obviously not intended for
seizing prey but for exertion of strength). The
molars are broad-topped and furnished at the top
with enamel folds to prevent waste caused by their

side motion, but not pointed for chewing flesh.

In omnivorous animals such as bears, on the other hand, the incisors resemble those of the herbivorous, the canines are like those of the carnivorous, and the molars are both pointed and broad-topped to serve a twofold purpose.

Now if we observe the formation of the teeth in man we find that they do not resemble those of the carnivorous, neither do they resemble the teeth of the herbivorous or the omnivorous. They do resemble, exactly, those of the frugivorous animals. The reasonable inference, therefore, is that man is a frugivorous or fruit-eating animal.*

Observation of the digestive canal. By observation of the digestive canal we find that the bowels of carnivorous animals are 3 to 5 times the length of their body, measuring from the mouth to the anus; and their stomach is almost spherical. The bowels of the herbivorous are 20 to 28 times the length of their body and their stomach is more extended and of compound build. But the bowels of the frugivorous animals are 10 to 12 times the length of their body; their stomach is somewhat broader than that of the carnivorous and has a continuation in the duodenum serving the purpose of a second stomach.

This is exactly the formation we find in human beings, though Anatomy says that the hu-

* Fruit comprises any part of plant life useful to man. The fruitarian diet referred to by Swami Sri Yukteswarji includes vegetables, nuts, and grains. *(Publisher's Note)*

man bowels are 3 to 5 times the length of man's body—making a mistake by measuring the body from the crown to the soles, instead of from mouth to anus. Thus we can again draw the inference that man is, in all probability, a frugivorous animal.

Observation of organs of sense. By observation of the natural tendency of the organs of sense— the guideposts for determining what is nutritious —by which all animals are directed to their food, we find that when the carnivorous animal finds prey, he becomes so much delighted that his eyes begin to sparkle; he boldly seizes the prey and greedily laps the jetting blood. On the contrary, the herbivorous animal refuses even his natural food, leaving it untouched, if it is sprinkled with a little blood. His senses of smell and sight lead him to select grasses and other herbs for his food, which he tastes with delight. Similarly with the frugivorous animals, we find that their senses always direct them to fruits of the trees and field.

In men of all races we find that their senses of smell, sound, and sight never lead them to slaughter animals; on the contrary they cannot bear even the sight of such killings. Slaughter- houses are always recommended to be removed far from the towns; men often pass strict ordi- nances forbidding the uncovered transportation of flesh meats. Can flesh then be considered the natural food of man, when both his eyes and his nose are so much against it, unless deceived by flavors of spices, salt, and sugar? On the other hand, how delightful do we find the fragrance of fruits, the very sight of which often makes the mouth water! It may also be noticed that various grains and roots possess an agreeable odor and taste, though faint, even when unprepared. Thus again, we are led to infer from these observations that man was intended to be a frugivorous animal.*

Observation of the nourishment of the young. By observation of the nourishment of the young we find that milk is undoubtedly the food of the newborn babe. Abundant milk is not supplied in the breasts of the mother if she does not take fruits, grains, and vegetables as her natural food.

Cause of disease. Hence from these observations the only conclusion that can reasonably be drawn is that various grains, fruits, roots, and— for beverage—milk, and pure water openly exposed to air and sun are decidedly the best natural food for man. These, being congenial to the system when taken according to the power of the digestive organs, well chewed and mixed with saliva, are always easily assimilated.

Other foods are unnatural to man and being uncongenial to the system are necessarily foreign to it; when they enter the stomach, they are not properly assimilated. Mixed with the blood, they

* "And God said, Behold, I have given you every herb bearing seed, which is upon the face of all the earth, and every tree, in which is the fruit of a tree yielding seed; to you it shall be for meat." —Genesis 1:29. *(Publishers Note)*

accumulate in the excretory and other organs not properly adapted to them. When they cannot find their way out, they subside in tissue crevices by the law of gravitation; and, being fermented, produce diseases, mental and physical, and ultimately lead to premature death.

Children's development. Experiment also proves that the nonirritant diet natural to the vegetarian is, almost without exception, admirably suited to children's development, both physical and mental. Their minds, understanding, will, the principal faculties, temper, and general disposition are also properly developed.

Natural living calms passions. We find that when extraordinary means such as excessive fasting, scourging, or monastic confinement are resorted to for the purpose of suppressing the sexual passions, these means seldom produce the desired effect. Experiment shows, however, that man can easily overcome these passions, the archenemy of morality, by natural living on a nonirritant diet, above referred to; thereby men gain a calmness of mind which every psychologist knows is the most favorable to mental activity and to a clear understanding, as well as to a judicial way of thinking.

Sexual desire. Something more should be said here about the natural instinct of propagation, which is, next to the instinct of self-preservation, the strongest in the animal body. Sexual desire,

like all other desires, has a normal and an abnor-
mal or diseased state, the latter resulting only
from the foreign matter accumulated by unnatural living as mentioned above. In the sexual desire
everyone has a very accurate thermometer to indicate the condition of his health. This desire is
forced from its normal state by the irritation of
nerves that results from the pressure of foreign
matter accumulated in the system, which pressure
is exerted on the sexual apparatus and is at first
manifested by an increased sexual desire followed
by a gradual decrease of potency.

This sexual desire in its normal state makes
man quite free from all disturbing lusts, and op-
erates on the organism (awaking a wish for ap-
peasement) only infrequently. Here again experiment shows that this desire, like all other desires,
is always normal in individuals who lead a natural
life as mentioned.

The root of the tree of life. The sexual organ
—the junction of important nerve extremities,
particularly of the sympathetic and spinal nerves
(the principal nerves of the abdomen) which,
through their connection with the brain, are capable of enlivening the whole system—is in a
sense the root of the tree of life. Man well-
instructed in the proper use of sex can keep his
body and mind in proper health and can live a
pleasant life throughout.

The practical principles of sexual health are

not taught because the public regards the subject as unclean and indecent. Thus blinded, mankind presumes to clothe Nature in a veil because she seems to them impure, forgetting that she is always clean and that everything impure and improper lies in man's ideas, and not in Nature herself. It is clear therefore that man, not knowing the truth about the dangers of misuse of the sexual power, and being compelled to wrong practices by the nervous irritation resulting from unnatural living, suffers troublesome diseases in life and ultimately becomes a victim of premature death.

Dwelling place of man. Secondly, about our dwelling place. We can easily understand, when we feel displeasure on entering a crowded room after breathing fresh air on a mountaintop or in an expanse of field or garden, that the atmosphere of the town or any crowded place is quite an unnatural dwelling place. The fresh atmosphere of the mountaintop, or of the field or garden, or of a dry place under trees covering a large plot of land and freely ventilated with fresh air is the proper dwelling place for man according to Nature.

The company we should keep. And thirdly, as to the company we should keep. Here also, if we listen to the dictates of our conscience and consult our natural liking, we will at once find that we favor those persons whose magnetism affects us harmoniously, who cool our system, internally invigorate our vitality, develop our natural love, and thus relieve us of our miseries and administer peace to us. This is to say, we should be in the company of the *Sat* or Savior and should avoid that of the *Asat,* as described before. By keeping the company of *Sat* (the Savior) we are enabled to enjoy perfect health, physical and mental, and our life is prolonged. If on the other hand we disobey the warning of Mother Nature, without listening to the dictates of our pure conscience, and keep the company of whatever has been des-ignated as *Asat,* an opposite effect is produced and our health is impaired and our life short-ened.

Necessity of natural living and purity. Thus natural living is helpful for the practice of *Yama,* the ascetic forbearances as explained earlier. Pur-ity of mind and body being equally important in the practice of *Niyama,* the ascetic observances already explained, every attempt should be made to attain that purity.

SUTRAS 12-18

ततः पाशक्षयः । १२ ।

घृणालज्जाभयशोकजुगुप्साजातिकुलमानाः पाशाष्टकम् । १३ ।

तदा चित्तस्य महत्त्वम् वीरत्वं वा । १४ ।

गार्हस्थ्याश्रमोपयोग्यासनप्राणायामप्रत्याहारसाधनेषु

        योग्यता च । १५ ।

स्थिरसुखमासनम् । १६ ।

प्राणानां संयमः प्राणायामः । १७ ।

इन्द्रियाणामन्तर्मुखत्वंप्रत्याहारः । १८ ।

Hence bondage disappears.

The eight bondages or snares are hatred, shame, fear, grief, condemnation, race prejudice, pride of family, and smugness.

(Removal of the eight bondages) leads to magnanimity of heart.

Thus one becomes fit to practice *Asana*, *Pranayama*, and *Pratyahara;* and to enjoy the householder's life (by fulfilling all one's desires and so getting rid of them).

Asana means a steady and pleasant posture of the body.

Pranayama means control over *prana*, life force.

Pratyahara means withdrawal of the senses from external objects.

The eight meannesses of the heart. Firmness of moral courage, when attained, removes all the obstacles in the way of salvation. These obstacles are of eight sorts—hatred, shame, fear, grief, condemnation, race prejudice, pride of pedigree, and a narrow sense of respectability—which eight are the meannesses of the human heart.

Awakening magnanimity of the heart. By the removal of these eight obstacles, *Viratwam* or *Mahattwam* (magnanimity of the heart) comes in, and this makes man fit for the practice of *Asana* (remaining in steady and pleasant posture), *Pranayama* (control over *prana,* involuntary nerve electricities), and *Pratyahara* (changing the direction of the voluntary nerve currents inward). These practices enable man to satisfy his heart by enjoying the objects of the senses as intended for *Garhasthyasrama* (domestic) life.

Value of *Pranayama.* Man can put the voluntary nerves into action whenever he likes, and can give them rest when fatigued. When all of these voluntary nerves require rest he sleeps naturally, and by this sleep the voluntary nerves, being refreshed, can work again with full vigor. Man's involuntary nerves, however, irrespective of his will, are working continuously of themselves from his birth. As he has no control over them, he cannot interfere with their action in the least. When these nerves become fatigued they also want rest and naturally fall asleep. This sleep of the involuntary nerves is called *Mahanidra,* the great sleep, or death. When this takes place, the circulation, respiration, and other vital functions being stopped, the material body naturally begins to decay. After a while, when this great sleep *Mahanidra* is over, man awakes, with all his desires, and is reborn in a new physical body for the accomplishment of his various yearnings. In this way man binds himself to life and death and fails to achieve final salvation.

Control over death. But if man can control these

involuntary nerves by the aforesaid *Pranayama,* he can stop the natural decay of the material body and put the involuntary nerves (of the heart, lungs, and other vital organs) to rest periodically, as he does with his voluntary nerves in sleep. After such rest by *Pranayama* the involuntary nerves become refreshed and work with newly replenished life.

As after sleep, when rest has been taken by the voluntary nerves, man requires no help to awaken naturally; so after death also, when man has enjoyed a full rest, he awakens naturally to life in a new body on earth. If man can "die," that is, consciously put his entire nervous system, voluntary and involuntary, to rest each day by practice of *Pranayama,* his whole physical system works with great vigor.

Life and death come under the control of the yogi who perseveres in the practice of *Pranayama.* In that way he saves his body from the premature decay that overtakes most men, and can remain as long as he wishes in his present physical form, thus having time to work out his karma in one body and to fulfill (and so get rid of) all the various desires of his heart. Finally purified, he is no longer required to come again into this world under the influence of *Maya,* Darkness, or to suffer the "second death." See I Corinthians 15:31, and Revelation 2:10, 11.

"I protest by our rejoicing which I have in Christ

[*consciousness*], *I die daily.*"—*St. Paul.*

"*Be thou faithful unto death, and I will give thee a crown of life....He that overcometh shall not be hurt of the second death.*"

Necessity of *Pratyahara*. Man enjoys a thing when he so desires. At the time of the enjoyment, however, if he directs his organs of sense, through which he enjoys, toward the object of his desire, he can never be satisfied, and his desires increase in double force. On the contrary, if he can direct his organs of sense inward toward his Self, at that time he can satisfy his heart immediately. So the practice of the aforesaid *Pratyahara,* the changing of the direction of the voluntary nerve currents inward, is a desirable way to fulfill his worldly desires. Man must reincarnate again and again until all his earthly longings are worked out and he is free from all desires.

Necessity of *Asana*. Man cannot feel or even think properly when his mind is not in a pleasant state; and the different parts of the human body are so harmoniously arranged that if even any minutest part of it be hurt a little, the whole system becomes disturbed. So to comprehend a thing, that is, to feel a thing by the heart clearly, the practice of the aforesaid *Asana,* the steady and pleasant posture, is necessary.

SUTRAS 19–22

चित्तप्रसादे सति सर्वभावोदयः स्मृतिः । १९ ।

तद्देवार्थमात्रनिर्भासं स्वरूपशून्यमिव समाधिः । २० ।

ततः संयमस्तस्मात् ब्रह्मप्रकाशकप्रणवशब्दानुभवः । २१ ।

तस्मिन्नात्मनो योगो भक्तियोगस्तदा दिव्यत्वम् । २२ ।

Smriti, **true conception, leads to knowledge of all creation.**

Samadhi, **true concentration, enables one to abandon individuality for universality.**

Hence arises *Samyama* ("restraint" or overcoming the egoistic self), by which one experiences the *Aum* vibration that reveals God.

Thus the soul (is baptized) in *Bhakti Yoga* (devotion). This is the state of Divinity.

Smriti, **the true conception.** Man, when expert in the above-mentioned practices, becomes able to conceive or feel all things of this creation by his heart. This true conception is called *Smriti.*

Samadhi, **true concentration.** Fixing attention firmly on any object thus conceived, when man becomes as much identified with it as if he were devoid of his individual nature, he attains the state of *Samadhi* or true concentration.

Pranava Sabda, **the Word of God.** When man directs all his organs of sense toward their common center, the sensorium or *Sushumnadwara,* the door of the internal world, he perceives his God-sent luminous body of *Radha* or John the Baptist, and hears the peculiar "knocking" sound, *Pranava Sabda,* the Word of God. See John 1:6, 7, 23.

"There was a man sent from God, whose name was John.

"The same came for a witness, to bear witness of the Light, that all men through him might believe."

"I am the voice of one crying in the wilderness."

Samyama, the concentration of the self. Thus perceiving, man naturally believes in the existence of the true Spiritual Light, and, withdrawing his self from the outer world, concentrates himself on the sensorium. This concentration of the self is called *Samyama.*

Bhakti Yoga or baptism, the second birth of man. By this *Samyama* or concentration of self on the sensorium, man becomes baptized or absorbed in the holy stream of the Divine Sound. This baptism is called *Bhakti Yoga*. In this state man repents; that is, turning from this gross material creation of Darkness, *Maya,* he climbs back toward his Divinity, the Eternal Father, whence he had fallen, and passing through the sensorium, the door, enters into an internal sphere, *Bhuvarloka.* This entrance into the internal world is the second birth of man. In this state man becomes *Devata,* a divine being.

SUTRA 23

मूढविक्षिप्तिक्षिप्तैकाग्रनिरुद्धाश्चित्तभेदास्ततो
जात्यन्तरपरिणामः ।२३ ।

Translation same as following commentary.

Five states of human heart. There are five states of the human heart: dark, propelled, steady, devoted, and clean. By these different states of the heart man is classified, and his evolutionary status determined.

SUTRA 24

मूढचित्तस्य विपर्ययवृत्तिवशाद् जीवस्य शूद्रत्वम्, तदा ब्रह्मणः
कलामात्रेन्द्रियग्राह्यस्थूलविषयप्रकाशात् कलिः । २४ ।

In the dark state of the heart, man harbors misconceptions (about everything). This state is a result of *Avidya*, Ignorance, and produces a *Sudra* (a man of the lowest caste). He can grasp only ideas of the physical world. This state of mind is prevalent in Kali Yuga, the Dark Age of a cycle.

The dark heart. In the dark state of the heart man misconceives; he thinks that this gross material portion of the creation is the only real substance in existence, and that there is nothing besides. However, this is contrary to the truth, as has been explained before, and is nothing but the effect of Ignorance, *Avidya*.

***Sudra* or servant class.** In this state man is called *Sudra,* or belonging to the servant class, because his natural duty then is to serve the higher class people in order to secure their company and thereby prepare his heart to attain a higher stage.

Kali Yuga, the dark cycle. This state of man is called *Kali;* and whenever in any solar system man generally remains in this state and is ordinarily deprived of the power of advancing beyond the same, the whole of that system is said to be in Kali Yuga, the dark cycle.

SUTRAS 25, 26

ब्रह्मणः प्रथमपादपूर्णत्वं द्वितीयसूक्ष्मविषयज्ञानाप्राप्तसन्धिकालं
        चित्तस्य विक्षेपस्तदा प्रमाणवृत्तिवशात् क्षत्रियत्वम् । २५ ।
ततः सद्गुरुलाभो भक्तियोगश्च तदा लोकान्तरगमनम् । २६ ।

Passing beyond the first stage in Brahma's plan, man strives for enlightenment and enters the natural *Kshatriya* (warrior) caste.

He is propelled (by evolutionary forces) to struggle (for truth). He seeks a guru and appreciates his divine counsel. Thus a *Kshatriya* becomes fit to dwell in the worlds of higher understanding.

The propelled heart. When man becomes a little enlightened he compares his experiences relating to the material creation, gathered in his wakeful state, with his experiences in dream, and understanding the latter to be merely ideas, begins to entertain doubts as to the substantial existence of the former. His heart then becomes propelled to learn the real nature of the universe and, struggling to clear his doubts, seeks for evidence to determine what is truth.

Kshatriya, the military class. In this state man is called *Kshatriya*, or one of the military class; and to struggle in the manner aforesaid becomes his natural duty, by whose performance he may get an insight into the nature of creation and attain the real knowledge of it.

Sandhisthala—the place between higher and lower. This *Kshatriya* state of man is called *Sandhisthala*, the place between higher and lower. In this state men, becoming anxious for real knowledge, need help of one another; hence mutual love, the principal necessity for gaining salvation, appears in the heart.

Motivated by the energetic tendency of this love, man affectionately keeps company with those who destroy troubles, clear doubts, and afford peace to him, and hence avoids whatever produces the contrary result; he also studies scientifically the scriptures of divine personages.

When man finds *Sat-Guru*, the Savior. In this way man becomes able to appreciate what true faith is, and understands the real position of the divine personages when he is fortunate in securing the Godlike company of some one of them who will kindly stand to him as his Spiritual Preceptor, *Sat-Guru*, or Savior. Following affectionately the holy precepts, he learns to concentrate his mind, directing his organs of sense to their

common center or sensorium, *Sushumnadwara,*
the door of the internal sphere. There he perceives the luminous body of John the Baptist, or
Radha, and hears the holy Sound (Amen, *Aum*)
like a stream or river; and being absorbed or
baptized in it, begins to move back toward his
Divinity, the Eternal Father, through the different
Lokas or spheres of the creation.

SUTRA 27

भूर्भुवःस्वर्महर्जनस्तपः सत्यमिति सप्त लोकाः । २७ ।

**The worlds or *Lokas* of creation are seven: *Bhu,*
Bhuvar, Swar, Mahar, Jana, Tapo, and *Satya.* (This
earth, and the "earthy" stage of man's consciousness, are called *Bhuloka.*)**

The Seven *Lokas.* In the way toward Divinity
there are seven spheres or stages of creation, des-
ignated as *Swargas* or *Lokas* by the Oriental sages,
as described in Chapter I:13. These are *Bhuloka,*
the sphere of gross matters; *Bhuvarloka,* the
sphere of fine matters or electric attributes; *Swarloka,* the sphere of magnetic poles and auras or
electricities; *Maharloka,* the sphere of magnets,
the atoms; *Janaloka,* the sphere of Spiritual Reflections, the Sons of God; *Tapoloka,* the sphere of
the Holy Ghost, the Universal Spirit; and *Satyaloka,* the sphere of God, the Eternal Substance,
Sat. Of these seven planes, the first three (*Bhuloka,
Bhuvarloka,* and *Swarloka*) comprise the material

creation, the kingdom of Darkness, *Maya;* and the last three (*Janaloka, Tapoloka,* and *Satyaloka*) comprise the spiritual creation, the kingdom of Light. *Maharloka* or the sphere of Atom, being in the midst, is said to be the "door" communicating between these two—the material and spiritual creation—and is called *Dasamadwara,* the tenth door, or *Brahmarandhra,* the way to Divinity.

SUTRA 28

भुवर्लोके ब्रह्मणः द्वितीयपादसूक्ष्मान्तर्जगत्प्रकाशाद् द्वापरः, जीवस्य
द्विजत्वञ्च, तदा चित्तस्य क्षिप्तत्वात्तस्य वृत्तिर्विकल्पः । २८ ।

Entering *Bhuvarloka* ("air" or "the world of becoming") man becomes a *Dvija* or "twice-born." He comprehends the second portion of material creation—that of finer, subtler forces. This state of mind is prevalent in Dwapara Yuga.

Dvija **or twice-born.** When man, being baptized, begins to repent and move back toward the Eternal Father and, withdrawing his self from the gross material world, *Bhuloka,* enters into the world of fine matter, *Bhuvarloka,* he is said to belong to the *Dvija* or twice-born class. In this state he comprehends his internal electricities, the second fine material portion of the creation; and understands that the existence of the external is substantially nothing but mere coalescence or union of his fine internal objects of sense (the negative attributes of electricities) with his five organs of sense (the positive attributes) through his five organs of action (the neutralizing attributes of the same), caused by the operation of his mind and conscience (consciousness).

The steady heart. This state of man is *Dwapara;* and when this becomes the general state of human beings naturally in any solar system, the whole of that system is said to be in Dwapara Yuga. In this *Dwapara* state the heart becomes steady.

If man continues in the baptized state, remaining immersed in the holy stream, he gradually comes to a pleasant state wherein his heart wholly abandons the ideas of the external world and becomes devoted to the internal one.

SUTRA 29

स्वर्गे चित्तस्थैकाग्रतया वृत्तिः स्मृतिस्ततः
ब्रह्मणस्तृतीयपादजगत्कारणप्रकृतिज्ञानवशात्
त्रेता, तदा विप्रत्वं जीवस्य । २६ ।

In *Swarloka* ("heaven") man is fit to understand the mysteries of *Chitta*, the magnetic third portion of material creation. He becomes a *Vipra* (nearly perfect being). This state of mind is prevalent in Treta Yuga.

The devoted heart. In this devoted state man,

withdrawing his self from *Bhuvarloka,* the world of electric attributes, comes to *Swarloka,* the world of magnetic attributes, the electricities and poles; he then becomes able to comprehend *Chitta,* Heart, the magnetic third portion of creation. This *Chitta,* as explained in Chapter 1, is the spiritualized Atom, *Avidya* or Ignorance, a part of Darkness, *Maya.* Man, comprehending this *Chitta,* becomes able to understand the whole of Darkness, *Maya* itself, of which *Chitta* is a part, as well as the entire creation. Man is then said to belong to the *Vipra,* or nearly perfect, class. This state of human beings is called *Treta;* when this becomes the general state of human beings naturally in any solar system, the whole of that system is said to be in Treta Yuga.

SUTRA 30

महर्लोके चित्तस्य निरुद्धत्वात्तस्य वृत्तिर्निद्रा
    ततः सर्वविकाराभावे ब्रह्मवत् स्वात्मानुभवात्
    ब्रह्मणत्वन्तदाब्रह्मणस्तुरीयांशसत्पदार्थप्रकाशात् सत्यम् । ३० ।

Through true repentance man reaches *Maharloka* (the "great world"). No longer subject to the influence of ignorance, *Maya,* he attains a clean heart. He enters the natural caste of the *Brahmanas* ("knowers of Brahma"). This state of mind is prevalent in Satya Yuga.

The Clean Heart. Man continuing Godward fur-

ther lifts up his self to *Maharloka,* the region of
magnet, the Atom; then all the developments of
Ignorance being withdrawn, his heart comes to a
clean state, void of all external ideas. Then man
becomes able to comprehend the Spiritual Light,
Brahma, the Real Substance in the universe,
which is the last and everlasting spiritual portion
in creation. In this stage man is called *Brahmana*
or of the spiritual class. This stage of the human
being is called *Satya,* and when this becomes the
general state of man naturally in any solar system,
the whole of that system is said to be in Satya
Yuga.

SUTRAS 31, 32

तद्रपि सन्न्यासान् मायातीतजनलोकस्थं मुक्तसन्न्यासी
तत: चैतन्यप्रकटिततपोलोकं आत्मनोऽर्पणात् सत्यलोकस्थं
कैवल्यम् । ३१-३२ ।

**Not merely reflecting but manifesting Spiritual
Light, man rises to *Janaloka,* the kingdom of God.**

**Then he passes into *Tapoloka,* the sphere of
*Kutastha Chaitanya.***

**Abandoning the vain idea of his separate exis-
tence, he enters *Satyaloka,* wherein he attains the
state of final release or *Kaivalya,* oneness with
Spirit.**

In this way, when the heart becomes purified,
it no longer merely reflects but manifests Spiri-

tual Light, the Son of God; and thus being consecrated or anointed by the Spirit it becomes
Christ, the Savior. This is the only way through
which man, being again baptized or absorbed in
Spirit, can rise above the creation of Darkness
and enter into *Janaloka,* the Kingdom of God;
that is, the creation of Light. In this state man is
called *Jivanmukta Sannyasi,* like Lord Jesus of
Nazareth. See John 3:5 and 14:6.

> *"Verily, verily, I say unto thee, Except a man be
> born of water and of the Spirit, he cannot enter into the
> kingdom of God."*
>
> *"Jesus saith unto him, I am the way, the truth, and
> the life: no man cometh unto the Father, but by me."*

In this state man comprehends himself as
nothing but a mere ephemeral idea resting on a
fragment of the universal Holy Spirit of God, the
Eternal Father, and understanding the real wor-
ship, he sacrifices his self there at this Holy Spirit,
the altar of God; that is, abandoning the vain idea
of his separate existence, he becomes "dead" or
dissolved in the universal Holy Spirit; and thus
reaches *Tapoloka,* the region of the Holy Ghost.

In this manner, being one and the same with
the universal Holy Spirit of God, man becomes
unified with the Eternal Father Himself, and so
comes to *Satyaloka,* in which he comprehends that
all this creation is substantially nothing but a mere
idea-play of his own nature, and that nothing in
the universe exists besides his own Self. This state

of unification is called *Kaivalya,* the Sole Self. See
Revelation 14:13 and John 16:28.

> *"Blessed are the dead which die in the Lord from henceforth."*

> *"I came forth from the Father; and am come into the world: again, I leave the world, and go to the Father."*

CHAPTER 4

विभूतिः THE REVELATION

SUTRAS 1-3

सहजद्रव्यतपोमन्त्रैः देहत्रयशुद्धिस्ततः सिद्धिः । १ ।
सद्गुरुकृपया सा लभ्या । २ ।
सहजद्रव्येण स्थूलस्य तपसा सूक्ष्मस्य मन्त्रेण
    कारणदेहचित्तस्य च शुद्धिः । ३ ।

**Adeptship is achieved by purification of man's
three bodies. It is also attainable through the grace
of the guru.**

**Purification comes through Nature, penance,
and *mantras*.**

**Through Nature there is purification of dense
matter (the physical body); through penance, purification of the fine matter (the subtle body); through
mantras, purification of the mind.**

Adeptship is attainable by the purification of
the body in all respects. Purification of the material body can be effected by things generated
along with it by Nature; that of the electric body
by patience in all circumstances; and that of the
magnetic body (चित्त *chitta*, spiritualized Atom,
Heart) by regulation of the breath, which is called
mantra, the purifier of the mind (मनः त्रायत इति
मन्त्रः). The process of how these purifications can

be effected may be learnt at the feet of the divine personages who witness Light and bear testimony of the Christ Consciousness.

SUTRAS 4, 5

साधनप्रभावेण प्रणवशब्दाविर्भावस्तदेव मन्त्रचैतन्यम् । ४ ।
देशभेदे तस्य भेदात् मन्त्रभेदः साधकेषु । ५ ।

Through the holy effect of the *mantra*, the *Pranava* or *Aum* sound becomes audible.

The sacred sound is heard in various ways, according to the devotee's stage of advancement (in purifying his heart).

By culture of regulation of the breath as directed by the Spiritual Preceptor (*Sat-Guru*), the holy Word (प्रणव, शब्द *Pranava* or *Sabda*) spontaneously appears and becomes audible. When this *mantra* (Word, *Pranava*) appears, the breath becomes regulated and checks the decay of the material body.

This *Pranava* appears in different forms at the different stages of advancement, according to the purification of the heart (*Chitta*).

SUTRA 6

श्रद्धायुक्तस्य सद्गुरुलाभस्ततः प्रवृत्तिस्तदैव

प्रवर्त्तकावस्था जीवस्य । ६ ।

One who cultivates the heart's natural love obtains the guidance of a guru, and starts his *sadhana* (path of spiritual discipline). He becomes a *Pravartaka*, an initiate.

It has already been explained what *Sat-Guru* is and how to keep the company thereof. Man, when endowed with the heavenly gift of pure love, naturally becomes disposed to avoid the company of what is *Asat* and to keep the company of what has been described as *Sat.* By affectionately keeping the company of *Sat* he may be fortunate enough to please one who may kindly stand to him as his *Sat-Guru* or Spiritual Preceptor. By keeping his preceptor's Godlike company there grows an inclination, *Pravritti,* in the disciple's heart to save himself from the creation of darkness, *Maya,* and he becomes *Pravartaka,* an initiate in the practices of *Yama* and *Niyama,* the ascetic forbearances and observances necessary to obtain salvation.

SUTRA 7

यमनियमसाधनेन पशुत्वनाशस्ततः वीरत्वमासनादिसाधने
योग्यता च तदैव साधकावस्था प्रवर्त्तकस्य । ७ ।

By the practice of *Yama* and *Niyama,* the eight meannesses of the human heart disappear and virtue

arises. **Man thus becomes a** *Sadhaka*, **a true disciple,
fit to attain salvation.**

It may be remembered that by the culture of
Yama and *Niyama,* the eight meannesses vanish
from the human heart and magnanimity comes
in. It is at this stage that man becomes fit for the
practice of ascetic posture and the other processes
pointed out by his *Sat-Guru* to attain salvation;
when he continues to practice the processes so
pointed out to him by his *Sat-Guru* he becomes a
Sadhaka or disciple.

SUTRA 8

ततः भावोदयात् दिव्यत्वं तस्मिन् समाहिते दैववाणी
प्रणवानुभवस्तदैव सिद्धावस्था साधकस्य । ८ ।

**He progresses in godliness, hears the holy *Aum*
sound, and becomes a *Siddha*, divine personage.**

On reference to Chapter 3 it will be found
how a disciple, while passing through the different stages, becomes able to conceive the different
objects of creation in his heart; and how he
gradually advances through the states of meditation; and how, ultimately, by concentrating his
attention on the sensorium, he perceives the
peculiar sound, *Pranava* or *Sabda,* the holy Word,
at which time the heart becomes divine and the
Ego, *Ahamkara,* or son of man becomes merged

or baptized in the stream thereof, and the disciple becomes *Siddha,* an adept, a divine personage.

SUTRA 9

तत्संयमात् सप्तपातालदर्शनम् ऋषिसप्तकस्य चाविर्भावः । ६ ।

Then he perceives the manifestations of Spirit, and passes through the seven *Patala Lokas* (or centers in the spine), beholding the seven *rishis*.

In the state of baptism (*Bhakti Yoga,* or *Surat Sabda Yoga,* absorption of the Ego in the holy Sound) man repents and withdraws his self from the external world of gross matters, *Bhuloka,* and enters into the internal one of fine matter, the *Bhuvarloka.* There he perceives the manifestation of Spirit, the true Light, like seven stars in seven centers or astrally shining places, which are compared to seven golden candlesticks. These stars, being the manifestation of true Light, the Spirit, are called angels or *rishis,* which appear one after another in the right hand of the son of man; that is, in his right way to Divinity.

The seven golden candlesticks are the seven shining places in the body, known as brain, the *sahasrara;* medulla oblongata, the *ajna chakra;* and five spinal centers — cervical, *vishuddha;* dorsal, *anahata;* lumbar, *manipura;* sacral, *swadhishthana;* and coccygeal, *muladhara,* where the Spirit becomes manifested. Through these seven centers or churches, the Ego or of man passes toward the Divinity. See Revelation 1:12, 13, 16, 20, and 2:1.

> *"And being turned, I saw seven golden candlesticks; and in the midst of the seven candlesticks one like unto the son of man.... And he had in his right hand seven stars."*

> *"The mystery of the seven stars which thou sawest in my right hand, and the seven golden candlesticks. The seven stars are the angels of the seven churches; and the seven candlesticks which thou sawest are the seven churches."*

> *"These things saith he that holdeth the seven stars in his right hand, who walketh in the midst of the seven golden candlesticks."*

In this state of baptism (*Bhakti Yoga* or *Surat Sabda Yoga*) the Ego, *Surat,* the son of man, gradually passing through the seven places mentioned, acquires the knowledge thereof; and when he thus completes the journey through the whole of these regions he understands the true nature of the universe. Withdrawing his self from *Bhuvarloka,* the fine material creation, he enters into *Swarloka,* the source of all matters, fine and gross. There he perceives the luminous astral form around his Heart, Atom, the throne of Spirit the Creator, provided with five electricities and with two poles, Mind and Intelligence, of seven different colors as in rainbows. In this sphere of electricities, mind, and intelligence, the source of all objects of senses and of organs for their enjoyment, man becomes perfectly satisfied with being in possession of all objects of his desires, and acquires a complete knowledge thereof. Hence the aforesaid astral form with its electricities and poles, the seven parts thereof, has been described as a sealed casket of knowledge, a book with seven seals. See Revelation 4:3 and 5:1.

"And there was a rainbow round about the throne."

"And I saw in the right hand of him that sat on the throne a book written within and on the back side, sealed with seven seals."

SUTRA 10

तदा ज्ञानशक्तियोगक्रमात्
सप्तस्वर्गाधिकारस्ततश्चतुर्मनूनामाविर्भावः । १० ।

Then, because of yoga knowledge and power, man obtains supremacy over the seven *Swargas* (heavens). He achieves salvation by dissolving the four original ideas (the "four *manus*" or primal thoughts by which creation sprang into being).

Passing through this *Swarloka,* the son of man comes to *Maharloka,* the place of magnet (the Atom), of which the ideas of manifestation (Word), Time, Space, and particle (Atom) are the four component parts. As mentioned in Chapter 1, this *Maharloka* represents *Avidya,* Ignorance, which produces the idea of separate existence of self and is the source of Ego, the son of man. Thus man (मानव, *manava*), being the offspring of Ignorance, and Ignorance being represented by the four ideas aforesaid, these ideas are called the four *manus* (मनु + ष्ण = मानव), the origins or sources of man.

SUTRA 11

ततः भूतजयादणिमाद्यैश्वर्यस्याविर्भावः । ११ ।

Being thus victorious over the powers of Darkness and Ignorance, man becomes one with God.

Maharloka, the place of Magnet (Atom), is the *Brahmarandhra* or *Dasamadwara,* the door between two creations, material and spiritual. When Ego, the son of man, comes to the door, he comprehends the Spiritual Light and becomes baptized therein. And passing through this door he comes above the ideational creation of Darkness, *Maya,* and entering into the spiritual world, receives the true Light and becomes the Son of God. Thus man, being the Son of God, overcomes all bondage of Darkness, *Maya,* and becomes possessed of all *aiswaryas,* the ascetic majesties. These *aiswaryas* are of eight sorts:

Anima, the power of making one's body or

anything else as small as he likes, even as tiny as an atom, *anu.*

Mahima, the power of magnifying or making one's body or anything else *mahat,* as large as he likes.

Laghima, the power of making one's body or anything else *laghu,* as light in weight as he likes.

Garima, the power of making one's body or anything else *guru,* as heavy as he likes.

Prapti, the power of *apti,* obtaining anything he likes.

Vasitwa, the power of *vasa,* bringing anything under control.

Prakamya, the power of satisfying all desires, *kama,* by irresistible will force.

Isitwa, the power of becoming *Isa,* Lord, over everything. See John 14:12.

> "Verily, verily, I say unto you, he that believeth on me, the works that I do shall he do also; and greater works than these shall he do; because I go unto my Father."

SUTRA 12

तत: सृष्टिस्थितिप्रलयज्ञानात् सर्व्वनिवृत्ति: ।
तदा मायातिक्रमे आत्मन: परमात्मनि दर्शनात् कैवल्यम् । १२ ।

**Knowledge of evolution, life, and dissolution
thus leads to complete emancipation from the bonds**

of *Maya*, delusion. Beholding the self in the Supreme Self, man gains eternal freedom.

Thus man, being possessed of *aiswaryas*, the ascetic majesties aforesaid, fully comprehends the Eternal Spirit, the Father, the only Real Substance, as Unit, the Perfect Whole, and his Self as nothing but a mere idea resting on a fragment of the Spiritual Light thereof. Man, thus comprehending, abandons altogether the vain idea of the separate existence of his own Self and becomes unified with Him, the Eternal Spirit, God the Father. This unification with God is *Kaivalya*, the ultimate goal of man, as explained in this treatise. See Revelation 3:21.

> *"To him that overcometh will I grant to sit with me in my throne, even as I also overcame, and am set down with my Father in his throne."*

CONCLUSION

"Love rules the court, the camp, the grove,
The men below and saints above;
For love is heaven and heaven is love."

The power of love has been beautifully described by the poet in the stanza quoted above.* It has been clearly demonstrated in the foregoing pages that "Love is God," not merely as the noblest sentiment of a poet but as an aphorism of eternal truth. To whatever religious creed a man may belong and whatever may be his position in society, if he properly cultivates this ruling principle naturally implanted in his heart, he is sure to be on the right path to save himself from wandering in this creation of Darkness, *Maya*.

It has been shown in the foregoing pages how love may be cultivated, how by its culture it attains development, and when developed, through this means only, how man may find his Spiritual Preceptor, through whose favor he again becomes baptized in the holy stream, and sacrifices his Self before the altar of God, becoming unified with the Eternal Father forever and ever. This little volume is therefore concluded with an earnest exhortation to the reader never to

* Stanza 2 from the third canto of *The Lay of the Last Minstrel,* by Sir Walter Scott.

forget the great goal of life. In the words of the illumined sage, Shankaracharya:

"नलिनीदलगतजलमतितरलं तद्वज्जीवनमतिशयचपलम् ।
क्षणमिह सज्जनसङ्गतिरेका भवति भवार्णवतरणे नौका ॥ "

["Life is always unsafe and unstable, like a
drop of water on a lotus leaf. The company of a
divine personage, even for a moment, can save
and redeem us."]

About the Author

Swami Sri Yukteswar, an ideal exemplar of India's ancient heritage of illumined *rishis,* is venerated as a Jnanavatar ("incarnation of wisdom") by people all over the world who have been inspired by his life and teachings. He manifested the self-mastery and divine attainment that have been the highest goal of Truth-seekers throughout the ages.

His Early Life

Born Priya Nath Karar in Serampore (near Calcutta) in 1855, Swami Sri Yukteswar was the only son of Kshetranath and Kadambini Karar. His father, Kshetranath, was a wealthy businessman, and the family owned several large estates in the area.

Even when he was a boy, young Priya's incisive intellect and thirst for knowledge were evident. As is often the case with great minds, however, he found formal education more of a hindrance than a help; his academic training was therefore not extensive.

Kshetranath Karar died when his son was still a boy. Consequently, at a very young age Priya Nath had to assume the responsibility of managing the family land holdings. In early manhood he was married, but his wife died just a few years later; and their only child, a daughter, passed away as a young woman not long after her marriage.

Priya Nath's pursuit of Truth led him to the great master Lahiri Mahasaya of Banaras, who extolled the sacred science of Kriya Yoga meditation as the most effective means of attaining God-realization, and who was the first to teach openly that ancient science in modern times. Through the guidance of Lahiri Mahasaya and through his own practice of Kriya, Sri Yukteswar achieved the supreme spiritual state, in which, as he describes in *The Holy Science,* "[one] abandons alto-

gether the vain idea of the separate existence of his own Self
and becomes unified with Him, the Eternal Spirit, God the
Father. This unification with God is *Kaivalya,* the ultimate
goal of man."

Writing of *The Holy Science*

Sri Yukteswar recognized that a synthesis of the spiritual
heritage of the East with the science and technology of the
West would do much to alleviate the material, psychological,
and spiritual suffering of the modern world. He was con-
vinced that tremendous advances could be made, both in-
dividually and internationally, by an exchange of the finest
positive features of each culture. These ideas were crystal-
lized by his remarkable encounter with Mahavatar Babaji, the
guru of Lahiri Mahasaya, in 1894. Sri Yukteswar told the story
of that memorable meeting as follows:*

> "Welcome, Swamiji," Babaji said affectionately.
>
> "Sir," I replied emphatically, "I am *not* a swami."
>
> "Those on whom I am divinely directed to bestow the
> title of *swami* never cast it off." The saint addressed me
> simply, but deep conviction of truth rang in his words; I
> was instantly engulfed in a wave of spiritual blessing. Smil-
> ing at my sudden elevation into the ancient monastic or-
> der,† I bowed at the feet of the obviously great and angelic
> being in human form who had thus honored me....
>
> "I saw that you are interested in the West, as well as
> in the East." Babaji's face beamed with approval. "I felt
> the pangs of your heart, broad enough for all men. That
> is why I summoned you here.
>
> "East and West must establish a golden middle path
> of activity and spirituality combined," he continued.

* Recorded by Paramahansa Yogananda in his *Autobiography of a Yogi,* ch. 36.

† Sri Yukteswar was later formally initiated into the Swami Order by the
Mahant (monastery head) of Buddh Gaya in Bihar. It was at that time that
he adopted the monastic name of Swami Sri Yukteswar ("united with God")
in place of his family name.

"India has much to learn from the West in material development; in return, India can teach the universal meth-
ods by which the West will be able to base its religious
beliefs on the unshakable foundations of yogic science.

"You, Swamiji, have a part to play in the coming har-
monious exchange between Orient and Occident. Some
years hence I shall send you a disciple whom you can train
for yoga dissemination in the West. The vibrations there
of many spiritually seeking souls come floodlike to me. I
perceive potential saints in America and Europe, waiting
to be awakened....

"At my request, Swamiji," the great master said, "will
you not write a short book on the underlying harmony
between Christian and Hindu scriptures? Their basic
unity is now obscured by men's sectarian differences.
Show by parallel references that the inspired sons of God
have spoken the same truths."

Returning to Serampore, Sri Yukteswarji began his liter-
ary efforts. "In the quiet of night I busied myself over a com-
parison of the Bible and the scriptures of *Sanatan Dharma*,"*
he later recounted. "Quoting the words of the blessed Lord
Jesus, I showed that his teachings are in essence one with the
revelations of the Vedas. Through the grace of my *paramguru*,†
my book, *The Holy Science*, was finished in a short time."

His Training of Disciples

As the years went by, Swami Sri Yukteswar began ac-
cepting disciples for spiritual training. His ancestral home in
Serampore became his hermitage; later he constructed an
additional ashram by the sea at Puri, three hundred miles
south of Calcutta.

It was in 1910 that Sri Yukteswar met the disciple whom
Babaji had promised to send him for disseminating Yoga in
the West: Mukunda Lal Ghosh, on whom Sri Yukteswar later

* Literally, "eternal religion," the name given to the body of Vedic teachings
that are the foundation of Hinduism.

† The guru of one's guru; in this case, Mahavatar Babaji.

bestowed the monastic name of Paramahansa Yogananda. In his *Autobiography of a Yogi*, Paramahansaji has described in detail his many years of spiritual discipline under Swami Sri Yukteswar, providing a fascinating biographical portrait of his guru, from which the following composite of brief excerpts is taken:

"Daily life at the ashram flowed smoothly, infrequently varied. My guru awoke before dawn. Lying down, or sometimes sitting on the bed, he entered a state of *samadhi*....*

"Breakfast did not follow; first came a long walk by the Ganges. Those morning strolls with my guru—how real and vivid still! In the easy resurrection of memory, I often find myself by his side. The early sun is warming the river; his voice rings out, rich with the authenticity of wisdom.

"A bath, then the midday meal. Its preparation, according to Master's daily directions, had been the careful task of young disciples. My guru was a vegetarian. Before embracing monkhood, however, he had eaten eggs and fish. His advice to students was to follow any simple diet which proved suited to one's constitution."

"Visitors appeared in the afternoons. A steady stream poured from the world into the tranquil hermitage. My guru treated all guests with courtesy and kindness. A master—one who has realized himself as the omnipresent soul, not the body or the ego—perceives in all men a striking similarity."

"Eight o'clock was the supper hour, and sometimes found lingering guests. My guru would not excuse himself to eat alone; none left his ashram hungry or dissatisfied. Sri Yukteswar was never at a loss, never dismayed by unexpected visitors; under his resourceful directions to the disciples, scanty food would emerge a banquet. Yet he was economical; his modest funds went far. 'Be comfortable within your purse,' he often said. 'Extravagance will bring you discomfort.' Whether in the details of hermitage entertainment or

---

* *Samadhi* (lit. "to direct together") is a blissful superconscious state in which a yogi perceives the identity of the individualized soul and Cosmic Spirit.

of building and repair work or of other practical concerns, Master manifested the originality of a creative spirit.

"Quiet evening hours often brought one of my guru's discourses: treasures against time. His every utterance was chiseled by wisdom. A sublime self-assurance marked his mode of expression: it was unique. He spoke as none other in my experience ever spoke. His thoughts were weighed in a delicate balance of discrimination before he permitted them the outward garb of speech. The essence of truth, all-pervasive with even a physiological aspect, came from him like a fragrant exudation of the soul. I was conscious always that I was in the presence of a living manifestation of God. The weight of his divinity automatically bowed my head before him."

"With the exception of the scriptures, Sri Yukteswar read little. Yet he was invariably acquainted with the latest scientific discoveries and other advancements of knowledge. A brilliant conversationalist, he enjoyed an exchange of views on countless topics with his guests. My guru's ready wit and rollicking laugh enlivened every discussion. Often grave, Master was never gloomy. 'To seek the Lord, men need not "disfigure their faces,"' he would say, quoting from the Bible.* 'Remember that finding God will mean the funeral of all sorrows.'

"Among the philosophers, professors, lawyers, and scientists who came to the hermitage, a number arrived for their first visit with the thought of meeting an orthodox religionist. Occasionally a supercilious smile or a glance of amused tolerance would betray that the newcomers expected nothing more than a few pious platitudes. After talking with Sri Yukteswar and discovering that he possessed precise insight into their specialized fields of knowledge, the visitors would depart reluctantly."

"Master numbered many doctors among his disciples. 'Those who have studied physiology should go further and investigate the science of the soul,' he told them. 'A subtle spiritual structure is hidden just behind the bodily mechanism.'"

* Matthew 6:16.

"'All creation is governed by law,' he said. 'The principles that operate in the outer universe, discoverable by scientists, are called natural laws. But there are subtler laws that
rule the hidden spiritual planes and the inner realm of consciousness; these principles are knowable through the science of yoga. It is not the physicist but the Self-realized master who comprehends the true nature of matter. By such
knowledge Christ was able to restore the servant's ear after
it had been severed by one of the disciples.'"

"Master expounded the Christian Bible with a beautiful
clarity. It was from my Hindu guru, unknown to the roll call
of Christian membership, that I learned to perceive the
deathless essence of the Bible....Never in East or West have
I heard anyone else expound the Christian scriptures with
so deep a spiritual insight as Sri Yukteswar's."

"Sri Yukteswar counseled his students to be living liai-
sons of Western and Eastern virtues. Himself an executive
Occidental in outer habits, inwardly he was the spiritual
Oriental. He praised the progressive, resourceful, and hy-
gienic ways of the West, and the religious ideals that give a
centuried halo to the East."

"Sri Yukteswar was reserved and matter-of-fact in de-
meanor. There was naught of the vague or daft visionary
about him. His feet were firm on the earth, his head in the
haven of heaven. Practical people aroused his admiration.
'Saintliness is not dumbness! Divine perceptions are not in-
capacitating!' he would say. 'The active expression of virtue
gives rise to the keenest intelligence.'"

"Sri Yukteswar's intuition was penetrating; heedless of
remarks, he often replied to one's unexpressed thoughts....
The disclosures of divine insight are often painful to worldly
ears; Master was not popular with superficial students. The
wise, always few in number, deeply revered him. I daresay he
would have been the most sought-after guru in India had his
speech not been so candid...."

"Amazing it was to find that a master with such a fiery

will could be so calm within. He fitted the Vedic definition of a man of God: 'Softer than the flower, where kindness is concerned; stronger than the thunder, where principles are at stake.'"

"I often reflected that my majestic master could easily have been an emperor or world-shaking warrior had his mind been centered on fame or worldly achievement. He had chosen instead to storm those inner citadels of wrath and egotism whose fall is the height of a man."

In 1920 Swami Sri Yukteswar sent Paramahansa Yogananda to America to carry out the mission spoken of many years earlier by Mahavatar Babaji — to make available to Truth-seekers throughout the world a knowledge of the liberating science of Kriya Yoga. For this purpose, Sri Yogananda founded Self-Realization Fellowship, an international society with headquarters in Los Angeles. During his three decades in the West, he lectured to capacity audiences in most of America's principal cities; wrote numerous books and prepared a comprehensive series of yoga lessons for home study; and trained monastic disciples to perpetuate the spiritual and humanitarian work entrusted to him by Mahavatar Babaji and Swami Sri Yukteswar.

In appreciation of his disciple's devoted service and accomplishments in America, Sri Yukteswar wrote to Yoganandaji on several occasions. The following extracts from two such letters, written in the mid-1920s, convey a poignant glimpse of the divine relationship of loving closeness that existed between these two great souls:

> Child of my heart, O Yogananda!
>
> I am melting in joy to see [the photos of] your yoga students of different cities. Hearing about your methods of chant affirmations, healing vibrations, and divine healing prayers, I cannot refrain from thanking you from my heart.
>
> * * *
>
> I am so glad to see the photo of the Mount Washing-

ton mansion* that I cannot possibly express it in words.
My soul desires to fly there and see it. You have worked
hard to be the instrument of God to create it. Carry on
the work as you wish. There can never be any difference
of opinion between us....

After I return to Serampore, I may try to get a pass-
port for a tour 'round the world, but conditions seem
that with this body it may not be possible to do so. I would
like to leave my body near you in your place. In that
thought I find great happiness.

About Puri, arrange as to who will take charge.
Through Guru's grace I am well. But I am taking leave
from all administrative matters connected with the various centers. I cannot accomplish all this detailed work
anymore. This is the beginning of my last efforts in connection with organizational work....I am waiting expec-
tantly for you.

His Last Days and Passing

As foreseen by Sri Yukteswar, it was not the will of the
Divine that he travel to America. Nor was Yoganandaji able
to wrest himself away from his manifold responsibilities in
order to visit India. Finally, in 1935, receiving an urgent intuitive summons from his guru — a portent that his guru's
days were drawing to a close—Yoganandaji returned to India
for a year-long visit. He was accompanied by two of his Amer-
ican disciples. The following account by one of them, Mr. C.
Richard Wright, provides one of the few personal descrip-
tions of Sri Yukteswarji written by a Westerner:

In grave humility I walked behind Yoganandaji into
the courtyard within the hermitage walls. Hearts beating
fast, we proceeded up some old cement steps; trod, no
doubt, by countless truth seekers. Our tension grew
keener and keener as on we strode. Before us, near the

* Reference to the Administration Building of Self-Realization Fellowship International Headquarters atop Mt. Washington in Los Angeles, which Paramahansa Yogananda had acquired a few months earlier.

head of the stairs, quietly appeared the Great One, Swami Sri Yukteswarji, standing in the noble pose of a sage. My heart heaved and swelled at the blessing of being in his sublime presence....

On bended knee before the master I gave my own unexpressed love and thanks; touching his feet, calloused by time and service, and receiving his blessing. I stood then and gazed into his beautiful eyes — deep with introspection yet radiant with joy....

I easily perceived the saintliness of the Great One through his heart-warming smile and twinkling eyes. Quickly discernible in his merry or serious conversation is a positiveness in statement: the mark of a sage — one who knows he knows, because he knows God. The master's great wisdom, strength of purpose, and determination are apparent in every way.

He was simply clad; his dhoti and shirt, once dyed an ocher color, are now a faded orange. Studying him reverently from time to time, I noted that he is of large, athletic stature; his body hardened by the trials and sacrifices of a renunciant's life. His poise is majestic. He moves with dignified tread and erect posture. A jovial and rollicking laugh comes from the depths of his chest, causing his whole body to shake and quiver.

His austere face strikingly conveys an impression of divine power. His hair, parted in the middle, is white around the forehead, streaked elsewhere with silvery gold and silvery black, and ends in ringlets at his shoulders. His beard and moustache are scant or thinned out, and seem to enhance his features. His forehead slopes, as though seeking the heavens. His dark eyes are haloed by an ethereal blue ring....In repose his mouth is stern, yet subtly touched with tenderness.

Though to all outward appearances Sri Yukteswarji's health appeared to be excellent, his time to leave the body was indeed drawing near. Late in 1935 he called Paramahansaji to him.

"My task on earth is now finished; you must carry on."

Sri Yukteswar spoke quietly, his eyes calm and gentle.

"Please send someone to take charge of our ashram in Puri," he went on. "I leave everything in your hands. You will be able successfully to sail the boat of your life and that of the organization to the divine shores."

The great guru entered *mahasamadhi* (a yogi's final, conscious exit from the body) on March 9, 1936, in Puri. The *Amrita Bazar Patrika,* leading newspaper of Calcutta, carried his picture and the following report:

> The death *Bhandara* ceremony for Srimat Swami Sri Yukteswar Giri Maharaj, aged 81, took place at Puri on March 21. Many disciples came down to Puri for the rites.
>
> One of the greatest expounders of the Bhagavad Gita, Swami Maharaj was a great disciple of Yogiraj Sri Shyama Charan Lahiri Mahasaya of Banaras. Swami Maharaj was the founder of several Yogoda Satsanga [Self-Realization Fellowship] centers in India, and was the great inspiration behind the yoga movement which was carried to the West by Swami Yogananda, his principal disciple. It was Sri Yukteswarji's prophetic powers and deep realization that inspired Swami Yogananda to cross the oceans and spread in America the message of the masters of India.
>
> His interpretations of the Bhagavad Gita and other scriptures testify to the depth of Sri Yukteswarji's command of the philosophy, both Eastern and Western, and remain as an eye-opener for the unity between Orient and Occident. As he believed in the unity of all religious faiths, Sri Yukteswar Maharaj established Sadhu Sabha (Society of Saints) with the cooperation of leaders of various sects and faiths, for the inculcation of a scientific spirit in religion. At the time of his demise he nominated Swami Yogananda his successor as the president of Sadhu Sabha.
>
> India is really poorer today by the passing of such a great man. May all fortunate enough to have come near him inculcate in themselves the true spirit of India's culture and *sadhana* which was personified in him.

His Legacy for Humanity

The awakened soul that comes into the presence of the Absolute knows God as the only Reality, and sees the transitory scenes of life and death as part of *maya*, illusion—a divine drama enacted in the omnipresence of the Cosmic Creator. After his passing, Sri Yukteswar gave to the world a profound last testimony to the truths he had so succinctly described in *The Holy Science*. As Yoganandaji, grieving over the loss of his beloved guru, made preparations for returning to America, Sri Yukteswar appeared to him in resurrected form. The wondrous experience—and Sri Yukteswar's revelations of the true nature of cosmic creation, of life after death, and of the continuing spiritual evolution of the immortal soul — is the subject of an entire chapter in Paramahansa Yogananda's *Autobiography of a Yogi*.

"I have now told you, Yogananda, the truths of my life, death, and resurrection," Sri Yukteswarji said to his beloved disciple. "Grieve not for me; rather broadcast everywhere the story of my resurrection . . . . New hope will be infused into the hearts of misery-mad, death-fearing dreamers of the world."

"Too long has [man] hearkened to the dank pessimism of his 'dust-thou-art' counselors, heedless of the unconquerable soul," wrote Paramahansaji in relating this divine experience with Swami Sri Yukteswar. By his life and the imparting of his wisdom, and by his death and the glorious demonstration of his resurrection, the great Jnanavatar bequeathed to all humanity a sublime vision of mankind's inherent divinity as immortal children of the one God.

Autobiography of a Yogi

By Paramahansa Yogananda

Autobiography of a Yogi is an absorbing account of a singular search for Truth, interwoven with scientific explanations of the subtle but definite laws by which yogis perform miracles and attain self-mastery. The author recounts his many years of spiritual training under Swami Sri Yukteswar, and his visits with exceptional personages of East and West—including Mahatma Gandhi; Luther Burbank; Therese Neumann, the Catholic stigmatist; and Rabindranath Tagore.

Dispelling many misconceptions about Eastern philosophy and religion, this book provides an excellent introduction to the whole science of yoga. Since its publication in 1946, *Autobiography of a Yogi* has become a classic in its field, revealing the underlying unity of the great religious paths of both East and West. It has been translated into 18 languages and is used as a text and reference work in colleges and universities throughout the world.

"There has been nothing before, written in English or in any other European language, like this presentation of Yoga."
—Columbia University Press

"A fascinating and clearly annotated study."**—Newsweek**

"A rare account."**—New York Times**

"As an eyewitness recountal of the extraordinary lives and powers of modern Hindu saints, the book has an importance both timely and timeless.... His unusual life document is certainly one of the most revealing...of the spiritual wealth of India ever to be published in the West."**—W.Y. Evans-Wentz,** *M.A., D.Litt., D.Sc.,*
Jesus College, Oxford

"Fragments of a wisdom so deep that one feels spellbound, permanently moved."**—Haagsche Post,** *Holland*

"Pages that will enthrall the reader, because they appeal to the aspiration and longing that slumber in the heart of every man."
—Il Tempo del Lunedì, *Rome*

"There are many books in Western tongues that expound Indian philosophy and particularly Yoga, but none other reveals to us with such candor the experiences of one who embodies and lives these principles."**—Kurt F. Leidecker, Ph.D.,**
Professor of Philosophy, University of Virginia

"This is a monumental work."**—Sheffield Telegraph,** *England*

Books by PARAMAHANSA YOGANANDA

Available at bookstores or directly from the publisher:

SELF-REALIZATION FELLOWSHIP
3880 San Rafael Avenue • Los Angeles, CA 90065-3298
TEL (213) 225-2471 • FAX (213) 225-5088

Autobiography of a Yogi
Man's Eternal Quest
The Divine Romance
Wine of the Mystic: *The Rubaiyat of Omar Khayyam—*
A Spiritual Interpretation
The Science of Religion
Whispers from Eternity
Songs of the Soul
Sayings of Paramahansa Yogananda
Scientific Healing Affirmations
Where There Is Light: *Insight and Inspiration*
for Meeting Life's Challenges
How You Can Talk With God
Metaphysical Meditations
The Law of Success
Cosmic Chants

Audio recordings of informal talks
by Paramahansa Yogananda

Beholding the One in All
Awake in the Cosmic Dream
The Great Light of God

Other books from the same publisher:

Only Love: Living the Spiritual Life in a Changing World
by Sri Daya Mata
Finding the Joy Within You: Personal Counsel
for God-Centered Living *by Sri Daya Mata*
God Alone: The Life and Letters of a Saint *by Sri Gyanamata*
"Mejda": The Family and the Early Life
of Paramahansa Yogananda *by Sananda Lal Ghosh*

A complete catalog of books and
audio/video recordings is available on request.

Free Introductory Booklet

Scientific techniques of meditation taught by Swami Sri Yukteswar,
including Kriya Yoga, are presented in Paramahansa Yogananda's
Self-Realization Fellowship Lessons. For further information, please
ask for the free introductory booklet *Undreamed-of Possibilities.*

INDEX

Lists references to main subjects, in English with Sanskrit equivalent (if applicable) in parentheses. For interested readers, a separate index of Sanskrit terms used in The Holy Science *begins on page 116.*

purification of man's three
bodies, 62, 70, 87–88

reincarnation, 46–47, 72–74
religions, unity of, 3–4, 6
repentance, 41, 52, 76, 81, 83,
91
Repulsion (outgoing creative
force of Spirit), 23, 26,
27, 29, 36, 48–49
Revelation, Book of, *v;*
quoted, 24, 25, 32, 34,
40, 43, 52, 56, 57–58, 73,
86, 92, 93, 96

sacrifice *(Yajna),* 55
salvation, 46, 53, 55–57, 59,
71–72, 79, 89–90, 93, 98.
See also emancipation.
Shankaracharya, quoted, 98
savior, 42, 53, 59–61, 85. *See
also* spiritual preceptor.
Scott, Sir Walter, quoted, 97
"second death", 73, 74
Self (soul), 22, 25, 34, 41, 43,
45–46, 48–49, 51, 52, 55–
57, 59–60, 74–75, 86
self-control, 62
Self-knowledge *(Atmajnanam),*
6
self-sacrifice, 43, 85, 97
senses, 18, 21, 29, 30–31, 34,
35–36, 37, 38, 39, 62–63,
65, 71–72, 74, 75, 79, 81,
82, 93
sensorium, 39, 75–76, 90. *See
also sushumnadwara.*

sex, proper use of, 68–69; desire, 67–68
sheaths *(Koshas),* covering
soul, 35–37
sleep, 38, 72–73
Son of God, 33, 38, 43, 53, 80,
85, 94. *See also Purusha.*
soul. *See* Self.
space *(desa),* 23–24, 93
spheres of creation *(lokas),*
32 ff., 80 ff., 91 ff. *See also
Sanskrit index: Bhuloka,
Bhuvarloka, Janaloka, Ma-
harloka, Satyaloka, Swar-
loka, Tapoloka.*
spiritual preceptor (guru), 39,
50–51, 58, 60–62, 78, 79,
87 ff., 97
stream, holy *(Aum),* 15, 40–41,
42, 52, 56, 76, 80, 82, 91,
97
study *(sravana),* 55, 79
subtle body. *See* astral body.
suffering, 45–47, 49 ff., 55, 57,
59 ff.

tenacity, blind *(abhinivesa),* 48–
49
time *(kala),* 15, 23–24, 93
Truth, 27, 35, 39, 55, 78–79, 97

virtue, 51, 56, 89

wakeful state, 38–39, 78
Word, the *(Aum). See* cosmic
vibration.

INDEX OF SANSKRIT TERMS

List of Sanskrit terms in the text, with English equivalent as given by Swami Sri Yukteswar. Some of the following terms are not discussed at length in the text, nor is their English rendering intended as a comprehensive translation of the Sanskrit. They are listed here for the convenience of readers particularly interested in Swami Sri Yukteswar's interpretation of Sanskrit philosophical terms pertinent to the context in which he uses them in this work.